PRAISE FOR *LEAD,*

Terry Cook's, *Lead, Develop, Care*, is perhaps the most significant book written on leader development in the past 15 years. This is not just another book on leadership theory or leadership flavor-of-the-month. This delightful work based on timeless principles, is intensely practical, easy to read and will help you become a different kind of leader, a trusted leader.

— *Jerry Forte, CEO, Colorado Springs Utilities, Ret.*

Life-changing. Terry outlines the timeless truths of leadership and makes them practical. Bravo!

— *Heath Wright, Chairman, Oklahoma Quality Foundation*

Using *Lead, Develop, Care* has allowed eight senior managers to quickly implement a consistent leadership program that has trained junior managers to develop and use individualized plans for our department resulting in consistently improving performance.

— *Luke Fox, Discovery Operations Manager, Division of Nelson Mullins Law Firm*

The LDC model and associated leadership coaching has helped our organization in so many ways. First and foremost, the LDC model provides an easy to understand and readily usable framework upon which to build and grow in all areas of leadership. LDC's focus on leadership development and being intentional about developing the right skill sets among our people has been a critical component of our success in building and maintaining strong, high-functioning teams. LDC offers the perfect combination of team coaching talent, program framework, and invaluable tools which has become an indispensable part of our strategic vision and a contributing factor in our success.

— *Jeff Delong, Executive Vice President and CIO, South State Bank*

The practical and teachable nature of *Lead, Develop, Care* allows me to develop leaders who will in turn develop more leaders. It's become the framework for me in my own leadership experience, inside and outside of the workplace. The focus on people and the clarity of the LDC model make this book an essential guide for any growing leader.

— *Jess MacCallum, President, Professional Printers*

Lead, Develop, Care has given me a framework I use to both improve as a leader as well as troubleshoot issues for myself and those leaders with whom I work.

— *Dave Kraft, Executive Coach and Leader Developer, Mission Viejo, CA*

Lead, Develop, Care has given me a lens to see and improve in my role as a husband, father, manager and leader.

— *Chapman Fairey, Segment Manager for Schaeffler Aerospace USA*

Lead, Develop, Care has given me the overall framework that allows me to hang all other leadership skills on.
— *Thad McAuley, Chief Operating Officer, Greater Europe Mission, Chantilly, France*

While working as a program manager for government-related contracts for major national intelligence organizations, I routinely use, think, and apply *Lead, Develop, Care* concepts. These principles provide me a foundation and framework for daily interaction with people to ensure work gets done effectively and efficiently.
— *Stan Burlingame, Principal Engineer, Fredericksburg, VA*

In my role as a team lead supporting Department of Defense organizations, I have been able to apply the *Lead, Develop, Care* framework to help equip and train members that had no past experience in their current assignments. As a result, they feel important and a valuable contributor to achieving our company's core goals and objectives.
— *Cheryl Burlingame, Programmer, Fredericksburg, VA*

Terry Cook's book takes the confusion and mystery out of being an effective leader by providing three key principles of leadership—Lead, Develop, and Care—and then providing ways to intentionally operationalize these three key principles. *Lead, Develop, Care* provides leaders with a mental model to assess their own leadership behaviors and determine what is needed to lead others in a particular situation. Ultimately, this book is about shaping a different type of leader—a trusted leader who is capable, competent, and successful in fulfilling their leadership responsibilities and bringing out the best in those they lead.
— *John A. Owen, EdD, MSc, Asst. Professor, Ret., Univ. of Virginia School of Nursing*

LEAD DEVELOP CARE

LEAD
DEVELOP
CARE

shaping a different kind of leader

THIRD EDITION

TERRY COOK

To Sherry—
Now and Forever.

To Paul Stanley—
Mentor, Colleague, Friend.
You started it all. Your legacy continues.

Lead, Develop, Care: Shaping a Different Kind of Leader

© 2020, 2021, 2024 Terry W. Cook

Third edition

LDN Publishing
1101 River Oaks Ln.
Charlottesville, VA 22901

www.ldnpublishing.com

Interior graphics by Luke Forister
Edited by Jenny Abel
Design and layout by Kelly Smith

Printed in the United States of America

Paperback ISBN: 978-1-7331319-5-7

Contents

Foreword

I had been given the responsibility to lead the Air Force Reservists in a major command of the United States Air Force. This command formed by combining two previous commands, making it the largest in the Air Force. But the merged commands were like oil and water. Their responsibilities and missions were very distinct. One had focused on research and development (this was the command from which I came), the other on logistics and sustainability. There was open hostility and resistance to the marriage of these two premier commands.

In the first meeting of my senior reserve leadership, I gathered about twelve brigadier generals and colonels—only half of whom I knew. The sense of resignation and apprehension in the room was palpable. As the meeting went on, I began asking these military leaders for input and suggestions on how we should work together and what our focus should be. I was met with silence. These men were, in the main, accustomed to the commander telling them what he wanted, giving the parameters and direction, and finally asking for any questions. In my leadership background with an international organization called The Navigators, however, I was used to robust discussion, friendly arguments, and shared ideas. My approach was not working in this new setting, though.

From that first meeting and subsequent ones, the leaders picked up on my refusal to give direction without their participation. That initially frustrated these senior reservists—all good, talented people (some went on to become one- or two-star generals) who were busy with their own careers as scientists, CEOs, corporate leaders, and more. They wanted to get things done and move on. No time for whipping up good feelings of camaraderie. Eventually, however, we began to develop a unified direction, supportive relationships, and trust. I began to coach each of them on their future, promotions, and work. Many became close friends with whom I keep in contact to this day.

How I wish I had known the full concept and directions of Terry Cook's excellent teaching in *Lead, Develop, Care* during my days with that command! What took us many years to build would have taken less time, with less frustration, no doubt. I had heard Paul Stanley talk about the Lead, Develop, Care model in our Navigator leadership meetings, but I had not really absorbed it, and most importantly, I did not apply it as fully as I could. Too often, I relied on my personal strengths, authority, and ideas to push people into action. Yes, I cared. But the three elements (Lead and Develop in addition to Care) were not always in sync.

In several decades of leading in a variety of situations, I have probably made every mistake imaginable. At times I have brought my military background, with its emphasis on authority, into play. As I modified that tendency, there have been times I did not lead strongly enough. If I had known the principles of *Lead, Develop, Care,* I would have avoided many mistakes and headaches. I began to read, observe good leaders, and be mentored. I also considered and even tried a number of fads found among the leadership teachings of the time. Terry Cook lived through many of those years with me. But he, building on the foundation of my dear friend and coworker, Paul Stanley, has created a model of leadership and leader development that really works. It not only works, but it honors both the leader and those being led.

Lead, Develop, Care is rich in both principles and practice. Terry offers a balance of the why and the how. Leadership according to this model is not one-dimensional; rather, it is an intersection of values, principles, and actions. That movement from ideas to action makes this book unique.

Does this book address every aspect of leadership? In one sense, yes—it provides an umbrella under which all leadership matters can be categorized. At the same time, of course, much has been omitted, as all books must do. Importantly, Terry maintains an action-oriented focus on how any leader, in any setting, can improve and grow.

This book is not just for CEOs. It applies to leaders at every level of an organization, from project teams to department leaders and executive teams. Throughout the model, the individual is given honor, real help, and encouragement.

This is outstanding teaching, combined with detailed practical methodology as well as a section on intensely usable tools.

Lead, Develop, Care will change you as a person, it will change your leadership, and it will greatly impact those who work for and with you.

Jerry E. White, PhD
Major General, U.S. Air Force, Ret.
International President Emeritus, The Navigators

Introduction

We are facing a crisis of epic proportions. It's a crisis of uncertainty—uncertainty about the future and uncertainty about those in leadership. It's also a crisis of hope—the loss of which is witnessed especially among the younger generations. This crisis isn't isolated to one country; it transcends national borders.

An article discussing a recent Barna study captures the nature of this crisis well. The article states:

> ... data show that young adults face some unique headwinds on their road to becoming effective leaders ... we hear a sense of unease about the future and uncertainty about the kind of leaders that could make a difference. Part of it is the underlying sense of anxiety that permeates many societies today. For good reason, the connected generation perceives deep, wide, systemic problems facing the world's future. Four out of five affirm—and nearly half strongly affirm—that "society is facing a crisis of leadership because there are not enough good leaders right now" (82%).[1]

My colleagues and I concur with these findings. Our experiences with leaders around the world over the past two decades point to the same conclusions. Good leaders are harder and harder to find.

The crisis of leadership is real, pervasive, and daunting ... but it's not hopeless! We believe that this time in history provides a unique opportunity to meet this crisis head-on. This book is about shaping a different kind of leader: the Trusted Leader. A leader of capacity and competence. One who serves others rather than uses others. One who not only gets results but also seeks to bring out the best in those he or she leads.

---

1 The Barna Group, "82% of Young Adults Say Society Is in a Leadership Crisis," *Millennials and Generations*, October 30, 2019; retrieved from https://www.barna.com/research/leadership-crisis. The article discusses "The Connected Generation," Barna's largest study ever, featuring more than 15,000 respondents in 25 countries and 9 languages.

The goal is not to load you down with a bunch of theoretical advice that you have no idea how to implement, but to give you practical guidance—enhanced by inspiring, real-life stories—so you can grow in competence and confidence as a leader. In short, I want to offer a framework that will take the mystery out of leadership. In the end, my hope is for you to become a Trusted Leader—the kind of leader others want to follow.

The framework presented in this book is a model for the everyday practice of leadership. It's for leaders of anything involving people: a home or family, a nonprofit, a team or club, a business, a health-care center or a school (and just about any other entity you can name). After you're done reading, I want you to be able to say, "I've got it, and I can use it tomorrow!"

This model is simple but not simplistic; it's easy to apply but also powerful in impact. It's a model that, if used consistently and correctly, will almost certainly change the entire culture of the organization you lead. This model doesn't guarantee a positive outcome or results, but it does offer a time-tested way of improving the people and relationships in your organization.

I wouldn't make such bold claims except that I've been a leader and have developed leaders within an international corporation for almost five decades; I helped create and have taught this model for almost fifteen years; and I can say without reservation, *it really works*.

My associates at **LDNGlobal** and I have brought this model to more than three thousand leaders from over seventy-five countries on all six populated continents. I've seen it work as well in countries like Kenya and Tanzania as it does in the United States or Europe. The model's clarity and practicality have been verified repeatedly in a wide variety of leadership situations.

LDNGlobal

When I use "we" or mention "my team" in this book, I'm speaking of an international network of leader developers who lead intentionally and developmentally.

This network represents:
• 18 key team members (since the model was fully developed)
• More than 575 years of collective leadership experience
• Thousands of leaders trained in the model since 1990

You can learn more about my organization at:
www.LeadDevelopCare.com

We have begun to track the effects of those who use this model. Recently, one of our European clients reported a significant decrease in staff turnover simultaneous with dramatic improvement in staff satisfaction. I'll be sharing similar success stories throughout this book.

Origins of the Model

Where did this leadership model come from? It comes from one of the oldest metaphors of good leadership in the Western world. The shepherd image appears as a picture of leadership in the writings that have survived from Assyria, Babylon, Egypt, Greece, and Palestine.[2] For example, you may recall the photo of the sarcophagus of Egyptian King Tutankhamun from around 1300 BC, with the shepherd's crook over his chest, symbolizing that he was like a shepherd in his leadership. In one of the most-read manuscripts in all of history, the Jewish Scriptures, we find the popular Psalm 23 written 300 years later. This well-known passage pictures God's leadership in shepherd terms. The culmination of this metaphor in the Bible is seen in the figure of Jesus, who is portrayed as the Good Shepherd who "lays down his life for the sheep."[3] Using these ancient manuscripts and concepts as a starting point, we found keys to both the "what" and the "how" of becoming a different kind of leader—a trusted leader.

My colleague, Paul Stanley, a West Point graduate, author, and international leader developer, came up with the rudiments of the model—Lead, Develop, and Care—in the mid-1980s. Another colleague, Tom Yeakley, author and leader developer, and I joined Paul in building out this leadership model from the core Primary Responsibilities of Lead, Develop, Care (or LDC) to the subsequent Operational Aspects and Tools & Exercises along with our seminar series and coaching format.

The LDC Leadership Model was also developed in response to a gap we kept seeing in the area of leadership training. We were traveling all over the world with the explicit charge of developing and training leaders.

There was another problem, too: Because the place we worked happened to be a service organization, the emphasis for leadership growth

---

2 Timothy S. Laniak, *Shepherds After My Own Heart* (Downers Grove, IL: IVP Academic, 2006).

3 John 10:11.

was placed primarily upon character development. Please understand, character development is critically important for effective leaders. However, just because a person has integrity and strong values doesn't automatically mean they're skilled as a leader. In fact, more and more, we noticed leaders whose competence was not commensurate with their strong character. Many of our trainees were wonderful people who had good intentions but were honestly unsure of how to order each day in such a way that they were not simply treading water.

Paul, Tom, and I decided together that *there must be a better way!*

During the 1990s and early 2000s, Paul, Tom, and I had been not only leading and developing leaders but also reading what other leaders had learned. We found this literature on leadership helpful and enlightening. We investigated various leaders from history, such as Abraham Lincoln, Dr. Martin Luther King Jr., Margaret Thatcher, John F. Kennedy, George Washington Carver, and William Wilberforce. I specialized in Winston Churchill, reading more books on him than on any other leader. We also devoured books by many of the prevailing experts on leadership, ranging from Stephen Covey (author of *The 7 Habits of Highly Effective People*) and Jim Collins (*Good to Great*) to Robert Greenleaf (author of *Servant Leadership*) and James M. Kouzes and Barry Z. Posner (co-writers of *The Leadership Challenge*), plus many more.

We discussed what we were learning. We all saw the same thing: a plethora of good leadership ideas, concepts, and techniques, but no single, unifying framework. It was as though leaders faced a thousand-piece jigsaw puzzle, with all the pieces strewn across the table in front of them, but no box-top picture to clue them in as to which pieces fit where.

We wanted something more—a solution that would be all-inclusive, yet simple. Thus, what Paul had begun we finished in what we now call the LDC Leadership Model.

Not Just Another Leadership Model

Across all our studies and experiences developing leaders, my team members and I have found a common phenomenon worldwide: many leaders struggle with their role of leadership. They may try to appear confident and sure of themselves from the outside, but on the inside, they feel unqualified or uncertain. A significant number would say they are barely hanging on, too busy and overwhelmed to even reflect on their own path of leadership. Still others find themselves on the "flavor of the month" treadmill, running from the latest leadership fad to the next.

We understand these struggles because we've seen them firsthand. So, let's be clear: This model is not just one more flavor to add to a menu of options. It's intended as a comprehensive, practice-oriented framework that can work in any leadership situation. We're not asking you to discard everything you know, but we are suggesting that anything you already know about leadership will almost definitely fit within this framework—and we think this simple model will make it easier for you to embrace and live your role as a leader.

This framework fits three essential criteria: it is values-based, culturally relevant, and functionally effective.

Values-Based

Great leaders throughout history, at their core, are tethered to a value or set of values greater than themselves; they aren't "in it for themselves," but are committed to noble values—values that, when lived, made them Trusted Leaders others wanted to follow.

Getting what you want through intimidation is a value, but it's not a noble one; it may produce a strong leader (think Hitler or Stalin), but it won't produce a Trusted Leader whom others want to follow. To the contrary, it's likely to result in fearful, disgruntled, even rebellious subjects.

As leaders, our values matter, and the specific values we choose influence our behavior—and those we lead—for better or for worse. The values at the root of our model are:

1. **Intentional**: Initiate with purpose, recognizing that good leadership doesn't happen automatically.
2. **Relational**: Connect with people, as they are your greatest asset as a leader.
3. **Incarnational**: Don't only speak the message; *be* the message. Being and doing must be intricately linked for trust to develop.
4. **Developmental**: Coach toward growth, because good leaders help those they lead to succeed.

Culturally Relevant

Given the cross-national span of our own work, we knew our model has to connect with all people in all circumstances. Every culture has its own peculiarities, customs, and nuances—assumptions about how things are done, about how people relate to each other, and about what is important and unimportant. Each leader is unique as well: No single leader has the same combination of personality, temperament, giftings, experiences, and cultural context. Our model transcends nationality and is usable to all leaders regardless of gender, ethnicity, age, language, or circumstance. It's not based on "American ways" of thinking, acting, and relating. (Indeed, even in America, there are a variety of cultural backgrounds and nationalities—the world is at our doorstep!)

Functionally Effective

Bottomline, the model *works*, in the real world, with real people. It's not just a system of lofty platitudes that inspire but leave one wanting in terms of practical application. It aims to help leaders succeed in their responsibilities while bringing out the best in the people and organizations they lead. It seeks to empower leaders so that, on any given day, they always know how to approach the question, "What should I do today?"

The Goal of This Book

By the end of this book, I hope you will both believe in the power of the Lead, Develop, Care model and see how you can incorporate it into your own leadership arena. I also hope this model will affect the results you desire as a leader each day, so that, ultimately, this model spreads to those you train (and beyond), transforming the landscape of leadership across the globe.

Chapter 1
The Big Picture

Jake looked like he'd had a rough night. In addition to adjusting to becoming a new dad at home, the young professional of a U.S. tech company had been tapped to lead a new project at work. To complete all the tasks he felt he needed to accomplish, he was spending fifty to sixty hours at the office each week.

This transition had caught Jake off-guard. He'd been a leader in the past: an officer in his college fraternity, an Eagle Scout in his younger days. A prolific reader, he devoured all the latest, top-selling books on leadership and management. His company had even sent him to several leadership seminars. But his mental landscape was, admittedly, foggy—scattered with a smattering of leadership advice and principles, but no clear vision of what to do next.

Jake's team wasn't making things any easier. He had always considered his teammates his friends. They had worked together with a sense of collegiality and even fun for several years, but since he'd been promoted, they treated him differently. Initial congratulations faded as they no longer treated him as "one of them." Some of his buddies outright resisted his leadership, refusing to cooperate.

As I talked with Jake over breakfast, I asked him to list some of his feelings on a piece of paper. The sheet filled with the usual adjectives: busy, overwhelmed, tired, confused, hurt. That last one, he added, was especially keen. He had overheard his colleagues gossiping about him behind his back, making comments like, "Looks like the position has gone to his head," and "He's not the kind of leader I was hoping he'd be."

Jake was grabbing any life buoy he could find to try to stay afloat, but nothing seemed to be helping. I pressed forward, asking him what model or approach he was using in his leadership role. He started, then hesitated, struggling for an answer. Finally, he conceded, "You know, I'm not quite sure I have a model. I guess I use a little bit of this and a little bit of that—whatever I think might be helpful at the moment." He added, a little sheepishly, "I feel like I'm blindfolded and groping in the dark for an idea, hoping the first one I grab will work, although I'm never quite sure."

"How successful has that strategy been?" I asked, though we both already knew the answer.

Foggy Thinking

In the example of Jake (based on a true story),[4] my friend genuinely wanted to know what he was supposed to be doing as a project leader; he wanted a fresh mindset and approach to his role. He just felt lost in the cafeteria of options.

In my experience working with leaders around the globe, I know Jake is not alone. In fact, my guess is, if you're reading this book, you share similar questions and struggles in your own leadership role. You may have a vague idea of how to lead, but when you try to articulate it out loud, you realize your idea is rather foggy.

If you're a leader, though, it's hard to lead a team forward while engulfed in fog. You need clarity of thought about what you are to *do* on Monday, Tuesday … and any other day of the week. You need to know, practically, how to implement your leadership role day in and day out. This is where a model comes in handy. It helps you see the way, rather than just "muddling through."

Why You Need a Model

I enjoy putting jigsaw puzzles together. Every piece is important. The puzzle is not complete if even one piece is missing. Yet, each piece that is pulled from the box lacks relative meaning and obvious placement by itself. I can hold it, examine it, turn it over, flip it around and upside-down, and still have no clue where it fits in the puzzle. I need something else besides that piece.

That *something* is the box top: the picture of the whole. I can then look

---

4 Most names of people used in examples in this book are pseudonyms for the sake of anonymity; in some cases, other details of their story have been altered for the same reason. In a few cases, a story is a composite of a couple of people for the sake of illustration.

LEAD DEVELOP CARE

at the distinctive features of each particular piece, compare them to the picture on the box top, and have a good understanding of where it likely belongs: "Ah-ha! This brown streak is part of the fence in the background on the right side!" The piece becomes useful as soon as you have this context.

Leadership principles and practices are like jigsaw pieces—helpful and needed if we know when and where to apply them effectively. But a leadership *model* does something more. It's like the box top, providing the "big picture" or overarching goal and vision for which the leader is striving.

> Model = a word picture or mental construct that is easily learned, remembered, and guides your thinking.

A leadership model is no good if it doesn't help with the practice of leadership. Through my team's seminars and coaching, we have discovered a foundational question most leaders are asking, and it goes something like this:

> "It's Tuesday [or whatever day]. What do I do?"

Too many leaders succumb to the tyranny of the urgent, from personnel demands to production quotas (on the family level, these might translate to number of beds and meals to make). In the smartphone era, this problem has been magnified exponentially. Many of us (not only leaders) are not only too busy, but too busy with the wrong tasks. And yet ... how do you know *which* tasks are the *right ones*? That is, which tasks will build momentum and work toward your final desired outcome? How do you bring out the best in the people you're leading, inspiring them to follow eagerly and not reluctantly?

I was conducting a leadership seminar for 400 university students in China and explaining the benefit of having a model. To see if they got the point, I asked them what they should do if, heaven forbid, their clothes should catch on fire. To my amazement, they immediately shouted out, "Stop, drop, and roll!" I don't know where they learned those three words, but learn them they did, and they had obviously internalized them. When you're being bombarded, a model enables you to focus on the essentials.

An Overview of the Model

At the center of the LDC Leadership Model are three words—Lead, Develop, and Care—which we call the Primary Responsibilities of leadership. If you get nothing from our model but these three concepts, you'll have a leadership framework that will serve you well for the rest of your life.

Why these three verbs? From our studies and experiences in leading and developing leaders, we concluded that these three are the absolute essentials of leadership. Many other responsibilities can be listed, of course, but upon closer examination, we think you'll find, as we did, that all others can find a home under one of these three umbrellas. Having a model with just three components makes it simple to remember (like "stop, drop, and roll") and therefore more useful.

One leader from whom we solicited early feedback on our model suggested that, while he liked the three components we had devised, he thought it was incomplete. He went on to propose nine other primary responsibilities. I responded by asking him if he thought he could remember and call to mind the twelve prongs of his framework on a daily basis, especially in a crisis moment. He quickly conceded that his model was too cumbersome to be of any real value. As the well-known quote, often attributed to Albert Einstein, goes, "Everything should be as simple as possible … and no simpler!"[5]

Here, we define the three Primary Responsibilities in brief for the sake of overview:

> **Lead = Intentionally influencing and enabling people to accomplish a given task.**
>
> **Develop = Intentionally strengthening people's capacity to grow and contribute.**
>
> **Care = Intentionally watching over and responding to people's needs and well-being.**

---

5 This quote may be misattributed, though some note that it could be a compressed version of something Einstein actually wrote.

We'll go into each of these in more detail in subsequent chapters. But for now, I want you to notice the one word common to all three definitions: *intentionally*. Intentionality is the connecting principle of our model. Good leadership doesn't just happen. It can't be only reactive, awakened in a crisis situation. For leadership to inspire a solid, trust-based relationship, it needs to be purposeful and planned.

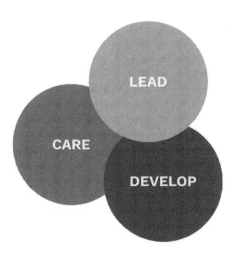

Equal in Importance, Unequal in Expression

As the graphic illustrates, with the three congruent circles, the three Primary Responsibilities are equal in importance and value. The "L" for Lead comes first in the name of the model partly just for a consistent nomenclature. But as we're about to see, it comes first for another reason, too.

Although the three Primary Responsibilities are equal in value, they are not equal in expression. How Lead, Develop, and Care are each manifested varies, and the amount of time, focus, and resources spent on each is different. The first question a leader needs to ask in any situation is, "What's needed now?" It's possible that one (or more) of the three Primary Responsibilities may be deficient at a given time and require the bulk of your current attention. In general, though, there is a normal, overarching pattern for employing the Primary Responsibilities in one's leadership role. That pattern is an 80%–15%–5% expression.

This ratio has been derived not so much scientifically but experientially. In other words, Lead should occupy about 80% of your thinking and efforts as a leader, Develop should take up roughly 15% of your time, and Care will capture around 5% of your attention. These proportions are estimates, of course, but through decades of study and experience, we've found that they're almost always best balanced in this manner *in a business setting*. (The percentages will vary in other leadership arenas. For example, a stay-at-home parent may find that Care requires 80% of their focus, while Lead takes the smaller slice of time.)

You're probably wondering how it is that we can still assert that Lead, Develop, and Care are equal in importance and value if they take up so much less time in a business leadership situation. Wouldn't this ratio suggest that Develop and Care are less important *in practice* in the workplace? Let me explain with an illustration.

Think of a favorite meal. Lead would be the main dish—your *entrée*. If you're a steak and potatoes person, it's the steak. If you're a vegetarian, it's the eggplant Parmesan casserole. Develop would be your side dish, perhaps mashed potatoes. Care would be your seasoning, such as salt.

Think about what would happen if you tried to serve this meal with equal amounts of each ingredient. Would you want a cup of salt to match the cup of potatoes? What would happen if you added that much seasoning? It would ruin the dish—you couldn't eat it. At the same time, if no seasoning is added, the dish would also be nearly inedible—or at least unenjoyable, a chore to swallow.

The 80–15–5 concept is similar and highlights two points about leadership.

First, the ratio is designed to show not how unimportant Care is but, rather, how powerful it is when even just a little bit is included. In the illustration of a meal, the right amount goes a long way. A small quantity seasons the whole dish and makes it tasty and pleasurable to eat. Too much, though, renders it inedible. When Care is present and done well in the right proportion, it is similarly compelling. The right amount, spread throughout the meal, flavors everything.

Second, the 80–15–5 concept demonstrates that if you are in a leadership role, your chief focus—the responsibility that takes up the bulk of your time—is Lead. Develop and Care will always play a role and be needed. One of them may even take precedence for a season. But ultimately, Lead is at the center—it's the mission.

Today, there seems to be an increasing aversion to Leading in the business sector; a more Care-centric focus has taken hold. The heart of true leadership must be recaptured by combining all three Primary Responsibilities, each in its proper proportion. In our seminars and coaching, we highlight the relationship between Lead and Care by stating "Care for your team by Leading well." It's not the other way around.

An Integrated Model

We've established that Lead, Develop, and Care are equal in importance but unequal in expression. One more key point is that, together, these three Primary Responsibilities form an integrated model. To be a Trusted Leader, you do have to carry out all three of the Primary Responsibilities. You can't just do one or two of them and neglect the third, asserting, "That's just not me." You need a minimum level of proficiency in all three for your leadership approach to be complete. Not one of them should be wholly delegated to someone else. In this sense, our model is an integrated model.

At the same time, most leaders will have a *strength* in one of the Primary Responsibilities—that is, one of either Lead, Develop, or Care will come most naturally to you. You're good at that one area; it energizes you.

You'll also likely have a *stretch* area. That is, with some work, you can carry out that responsibility quite well. It's not quite as natural as your strength, but you can be effective in executing it.

Finally, most leaders will have a *struggle* in the third area (and some will struggle in two of the Primary Responsibilities). In other words, either leading, developing, or caring will feel less natural for you. To be intentional in that area, you'll have to put forth some real effort.

A strength, a stretch, and a struggle. It's important to identify your own.

Sure, the rare leader will have a strength in two or even all three of the Primary Responsibilities, but these cases will be the exception rather than the rule. Good leaders aren't necessarily good because everything about leadership comes naturally to them; good leaders know their weaknesses, are willing to work on them, and also know how to help shore them up by utilizing the strengths of others.

You may be wondering why our model is integrated; in other words, why do all three Primary Responsibilities need to be in operation for trust to occur? Well, let's consider what happens when one of these areas goes missing. Here are three scenarios.

Deficient in Care

If you only lead and develop but don't care, people will feel unimportant and neglected.

When I worked on Capitol Hill, one of my friends mentioned that he had worked in his Senator's office for more than two years, and the Senator still didn't even know his name. I asked him how that made him feel. "Like a cog in a machine," he replied. Shortly thereafter he took a job in another government agency.

A recent Randstad USA survey sought to answer the question, "Why do people quit their jobs?" They found that 59 percent of respondents felt their companies view profit or revenue as more important than how people are treated.[6] Respect and care in the workplace really matter.

Deficient in Lead

If you develop and care but don't lead, people will feel important, but nothing will get accomplished.

One of the leaders I was coaching in Europe had a strength in caring. I mentioned to him one day that, while his team all felt really cared for, they were also very frustrated with him. He acknowledged their frustration but couldn't understand why they felt the way they did, especially after all the hospital visits and meals he prepared when they were sick. I shared that the reason they were frustrated was not due to his lack of genuine concern for them, but to the fact that, as the team leader, he wasn't taking them anywhere. They weren't moving toward a defined goal. Consequently, he had a history of staff turnover about every two years. This

---

6 Randstad North America, "Your Best Employees Are Leaving. But Is It Personal or Practical?" (press release, August 28, 2018), accessed April 6, 2019, at randstadusa.com/business/business-insights/employee-retention/your -best-employees-are-leaving-it-personal-practical.

constant change to his team was wreaking havoc for myriad reasons.

Deficient in Develop

Finally, if you care and lead but do not develop, people stagnate and underperform. You basically mortgage the future.

Younger workers today especially value their own personal and professional development. There's also a trend among the younger generation to move from job to job. Typically, the reason cited for such frequent employment changes is a greater potential for growth and development in another job than in the previous one. Of course, it's not only young people looking for growth. Workers of all ages and stages want to achieve to their highest potential. In the same Randstad USA survey cited previously, 58 percent of respondents reported that they didn't feel their companies had enough growth opportunities in the long term for them to stay, and 57 percent said they needed to leave their current workplaces to take their careers to the next level.

The End of the Story

One of the most exciting things about our model is its ability to provide clarity and hope. Remember foggy-minded, disillusioned Jake from the beginning of this chapter? I shared our leadership model with him shortly after the conversation mentioned earlier. He responded with great enthusiasm. In fact, as I explained the model to him, he practically shouted, "This makes sense! I get it, and I can use it now." After months of ongoing coaching, Jake began to see a shift in his team's response to him. As he began to lead, develop, and care for them well, they began to appreciate him and the new kind of leadership he was providing. He said he was even beginning to look forward to going to work. We hear these types of testimonials all the time, and we hope you will become one of them!

When we discuss Develop more in-depth in chapter 3, we'll discuss why, oftentimes, it's simply wrong assumptions on the part of the leader that hamper this area of responsibility. One of those assumptions is that developing workers is the same thing as giving them a lot of experience, but they're not necessarily equivalent.

Neglect a Responsibility at Your Peril

All of us can be blinded by our strengths, thinking they will surely compensate for any minor leadership struggles we have (minor, at least, in our eyes!). Those you lead may very well appreciate your strengths, and those may impel them to "hang in there" for a time. But eventually, the deficiency (or deficiencies) will be seen, felt, and acted upon. That is because all three of the Primary Responsibilities truly are essential for you to carry out and for those you lead to experience.

Next Steps

Now that you (I hope) see the need for a model in general and have a sense of the LDC Leadership Model in particular, it's time to look deeper at what the three Primary Responsibilities entail—and how to put them into practice.

For the rest of this book, I'll be taking you deeper into each Primary Responsibility:

- In **part I**, I'll define each more completely so that you have a firm grasp on each component of the LDC Leadership Model and how they relate.

- Then, in **part II**, I'll move into the implementation side of each responsibility. In the expanded diagram found in that section, a ring is shown around each of the three Primary Responsibilities. Those rings contain what we call the Operational Aspects. These are the three or four aspects involved in "operationalizing" (or implementing) each of the three Primary Responsibilities.

- Finally, in **part III**, I'll provide a robust set of practical tools and exercises that will get you started with incorporating the model into your own leadership situation. These tools can be used more than once and as ongoing "checkups," so that you continue applying the model over time (after all, this model is not something you apply once—it's something you will apply for the rest of your life).

My goal is your success as a leader. I hope you will see that goal beginning to be realized—or realized to a greater extent than it is now—by the time you finish reading. Ready? Let's dig in.

Chapter 1 Key Takeaways:

- The LDC Leadership Model is composed of three Primary Responsibilities: Lead, Develop, and Care.
- All three of these responsibilities are necessary for every leader, but every leader usually has a strength in one area, a stretch in another area, and a struggle in the third area.
- This model provides a framework for leadership and doesn't ask you to discard everything else you've learned about leading.

Part I
The Primary Responsibilities

I asked one leader how he thought his leadership was going. He paused for a second or two and replied, "Well, I'll have to wait until I get into the office and see what's in my inbox."

Whether he realized it or not, this leader was verbalizing a common perspective of leaders around the world—namely, that leadership is primarily a reactionary role. As another leader put it, "Leadership is learning to handle whatever is thrown at you. And believe me, they throw a lot of stuff at the leader."

Leaders do have to respond to things. Situations pop up. Circumstances change. People find themselves in a bind. A question needs an answer. And critics are never unemployed. The buck stops with you when these things happen.

Yet, leadership is about much more than reacting to the difficult or the unexpected. Leadership is (or, at least, should be) proactive. Good leaders make things happen through intentional leading, developing, and caring for others. Out of all the things you could be doing as a leader, our model contends that, at minimum, these three must be done. Why these three and what do we mean by them? That's what the next three chapters are all about.

Chapter 2
Primary Responsibility #1: Lead

*It was early in the morning, especially for the thirteen new college grad-
uates sitting around the table facing me. Most were from Ivy League
schools. Bright. Intelligent. Gifted. And still a bit sleepy. I smiled to myself
thinking how this introduction to the workday world must stand in stark
contrast to their schedules for the past four years. I was also hoping the
caffeine from the coffee would kick in soon.*

*All of these twentysomethings were part of a one-year internship for
young leaders. Each was placed in a service organization in my community, but I was here to help them learn how to lead, whatever their setting.
Our topic for today, officially, was "A Different Kind of Leader."*

*After brief introductions, I asked for a show of hands to a simple question:
"How many of you aspire to leadership?"*

*Can you guess how many of those Princeton, Harvard, Yale, and North
Texas graduates (OK, maybe my alma mater was not represented by any
of them) raised their hands? Not a single one. Even with their academic
pedigrees, their well-documented leadership experiences at a top-notch
university, and their selection for this one-year leadership program, not
one indicated an aspiration to be a leader.*

*Leaders and leadership have become disquieting concepts, especially to the
younger generation. These young interns validated their response by reciting
a plethora of examples of bad leaders in virtually every facet of society. The
solution, in their view, was to just avoid leadership completely.*

*As I probed further, one intern finally conceded, "If I have to lead, I'll lead
without authority." I know what she was saying. She wasn't going to abuse
others in her leadership position. I asked her, "Can a person lead without
authority?" After a pause with no answer, I said, "I would suggest that
you cannot lead without authority. The question is not how to lead without authority but how to use authority effectively. As we go through this*

course, I'm going to challenge you to rethink your perception of leaders, leadership, and authority."

Why did I challenge those young adults? Because we've given up some critically important concepts. We must recapture them.

Leaders have to lead; this is a redundancy in terms and, thus, obviously not an option! Leading is both a great adventure as well as a sobering responsibility. But what does it mean to lead—what does leading entail?

Leading is not merely moderating. It's not facilitating. And it's not just being a coordinator. Good leadership is active. It implies an authority and power to take action to make things happen.

Defining Lead

Here's our model's basic definition of Lead:

> **Lead = Intentionally influencing and enabling people to accomplish a given task**

Words are important, especially in definitions, so let's break down each key term to get a full grasp on this first Primary Responsibility.

Intentionally

Woven throughout our model, intentionality involves purposefulness and deliberateness. It means being proactive, not reactive. It carries the familiar concept of "stepping up," or taking the initiative.

One wife in a leadership symposium raised her hand quickly in response to my question related to why intentionality or initiative is so important in leadership. To the embarrassment of her husband seated next to her, she shared how her husband tended to lead the family like a first responder, like a fireman—meaning, he didn't usually step up to lead until a situation reached the level of crisis. By then, she went on, the fire is blazing, emotions are high, voices are raised, kids are crying, and peaceful and helpful resolutions are next to impossible. I could see the frustration in her eyes as she closed with, "By the time he tries to lead, the pin has been pulled, the grenade has exploded, and the damage has been done." Rather than leading their family in the situations it faced, she was suggesting, her husband was being led by them; he was reactive.

Intentionality is more than stepping up to the situation at hand. It also involves getting ahead of future situations. It means taking time to assess, think, and plan.

I often suggest to executives whom I coach that they take three hours out of their busy work week to reflect on what happened that week and what subsequently needs to happen the next week; then, plan accordingly, I urge them. Weekly reflection is a first step toward becoming proactive rather than reactive—and this is a great practice for anyone, from a spouse or parent to an employee or student. Often, the initial reaction of these executives is to ask a question like, "How can I afford to take *three* whole hours to reflect and plan?" My response is always the same: "How can you *not* afford the time?" Often, this reflection and planning time has the effect of *saving* precious time from being wasted the following week, plus makes everything else go more smoothly. Whether it's one, two, three, or even more hours, a regular time devoted to reflection is vital for becoming more intentional as a leader.

Influencing

Influencing means having the power to affect. Our oldest daughter and her husband were visiting us with their black Labrador Retriever named Hunter. I let Hunter outside when he suddenly saw a deer and took off after it. I yelled "Hunter!" several times. What did Hunter do? He kept chasing the deer. At that same moment, my son-in-law stepped outside and saw what was happening. He yelled "Hunter!" just as I had done. Hunter stopped in his tracks immediately. Why? Because my son-in-law was Hunter's owner who had raised him from a pup. He had the power to affect. We may have been on my property, but that didn't matter; I didn't have the power to influence Hunter regardless of where we were or how authoritatively I tried to yell.

There are leaders who may have a certain title or position that carries the idea of authority, but who, in actuality, lack the power to influence. This may be because of the lack of a relationship, the lack of competence, a checkered history, or some other factor that causes those they lead not to be affected by them. Without influence, a leader—indeed, the entire team—won't get very far.

Enabling

Enabling means "helping to make possible." Leading is more than influence. Because leading is linked to task (the final term in our definition), leaders need to not only influence people toward a task but help them be successful in accomplishing that task. Many a leader steps into a leadership role and has a dazzling vision. Yet, failure results if his or her words can't make it out of the theoretical realm. Leaders have to go beyond an inspirational challenge to actually equipping those they lead to fulfill that challenge.

We saw the importance of enabling firsthand with one of our clients. The executive director pronounced a new vision of expanding his organization into numerous cities over the next few years. He promoted his vision everywhere he went. This was going to take the organization to new heights. It was quite a plan, I had to admit. However, it never came to fruition. Why? He never enabled those under him to make the vision reality, primarily because there was no funding, no recruiting, and no training to make it happen. Talk about a "bricks without straw" scenario. It didn't matter how successful this leader was at getting people to embrace his vision, as his influence wasn't matched by the resources he needed to supply them to *enable* them to realize that vision.

People

As Dr. Henry Cloud points out in *Boundaries for Leaders*, leadership is all about people. There can be sixteen different strategies and plans for accomplishing the mission and vision of a company or organization, and most of them have the potential to work. The essential factor is the people who will utilize those strategies. Many leaders lose sight of this reality in the organizational culture of their company. They see titles, positions, charts, spreadsheets, processes, and physical plants, but they fail to see that it's ultimately the people who carry out the organization's mission. Valuing and bringing out the best in people is therefore an essential aspect of leading.

There has to be more than lip service, too. I've never met an executive who *said* he did not value his employees. Yet, in survey after survey, employees complain that they feel undervalued at work.[7] One such office in

---

7 For example, the American Psychological Association's 2012 survey, summarized at www.apa.org/news/press/releases/2012/03/well-being.

the Middle East was a sad illustration. Good employees were consistently bailing out of one director's office—for years, this pattern continued. Yet, Jameel was quite adamant that the problem wasn't him; he had demonstrated great care for his staff, he contended, through a job, good pay, and benefits. He couldn't understand why team members kept leaving, and he continued to chalk up his situation to bad luck. But interviewing any of Jameel's former employees revealed the true nature of his leadership. They had felt like names on an organizational chart, there with one purpose and one purpose only: to get a job done … for him. Jameel never *felt* he was undervaluing his employees, but his words and actions spoke otherwise. It took a lot of coaching over time for him to recognize that his view of people was one thing in his mind and another in practice.

Accomplish

I'm sure we all know leaders whose words are louder than their actions; their talk and accomplishment don't match. Results do matter. It's not enough merely to inspire, to say the right things, and to supply the necessary resources. Goals and targets need to be met.

I was working with some executives who had hired a man as the development officer, charged with raising money for the organization. At his introduction, this new hire talked a really good game. He shared his credentials, his experience, and his vision for how he was going to raise the needed funds for the group. Everyone was encouraged with his presentation. A year later, I was at the same annual meeting listening to the CEO share that not only had this man not raised the needed funds, but the organization was almost $100,000 in the red due to the expenditures of this development director. He was let go (and rightfully so).

In non-workplace and noncompetitive settings, the "results" of leadership can be harder to see and define. Parents, for example, know they don't just want larger versions of today's toddlers—they want to see steady, positive progress from their leadership over time. But what does "accomplishing" look like in a home or similar setting?

I was on a ski chairlift in Vail, Colorado, when I had the following exchange with a man named Vance, a doctor, who had recently moved his family from a large Pacific Northwest city to Vail because he wanted his kids to "grow up right."

"I commend you for making your family a priority," I told him, then followed with this question: "What do you think that looks like, to 'grow up right'?"

"What do you mean?" Vance asked me.

I rephrased the question: "What will need to take place in your kids for you to be able to say your goal was accomplished?"

Vance stared across the Rockies and finally replied, "I guess I haven't really thought that through in much detail."

"Do you mind if I throw out some suggestions?" I asked. When he nodded for me to continue, I rattled off a few ideas: "Successful parenting means our kids become aware of who they are, including their gifts, strengths, and weaknesses, and how to make their best contributions with those; that they know how to manage themselves well and take responsibility for their actions; they learn to respect and value people; they learn the importance of family and team, and how to relate well with others; and they learn to handle disappointments in life in positive ways."

As Vance and I neared the top of the mountain, he smiled, grabbed my hand, and gave a hearty thanks before stepping off the chairlift.

Given

This word refers to a task that is mutually agreed upon and understood. This is where many leaders fail: They assume that everyone is on the same page and understands the end goal.

If you have (or have ever had) a teenager at home, you can probably identify. You go into your daughter's room, stepping over clothes, books, notebooks, boxes, pillows, and other land mines on the floor. You say to her, "Honey, you need to clean your room." She argues at first and then reluctantly says, "FINE, I'll clean it up." You come back an hour later and find the room in basically the same state. You query her: "I thought I told you to clean up your room!" And how does she respond? "I did!" What's the problem? You and your daughter had different definitions of what a clean room looks like. The "given" was assumed rather than clarified and agreed upon.

I see many leaders get frustrated with their direct reports for not accomplishing a particular task, when the problem lies (at least in part) with their own failure to clearly communicate their expectations. If your daughter doesn't know the definition of a successfully cleaned room, or your direct report doesn't know what a successfully executed event looks like, then you've overlooked this need to clarify the "given."

Task

Lastly, leading others always involves a task. This is where leadership starts. Without a task, a leader is not needed.

To demonstrate this point in our leadership symposia, the seminar presenter asks everyone in the room to stand with their table group. They are told to look at the others at their table for twenty awkward seconds without saying a word. Then, the presenter instructs each of the groups to line up in order of age, from oldest to youngest. Instantly, in each group, someone leaps into action. The "leader" starts asking how old each person is. She grabs her tablemate by the arm and directs him to the appropriate position in the line. In a matter of seconds, each table has the correct alignment. The interesting thing is that no one asked or authorized that particular person to take action. He or she just reacted to the task at hand. No leader was needed at the tables while they were just standing there for those twenty seconds of silence. Once the task is given, a leader is revealed.

There's no dearth of books on leadership and management in the world. Whether in print or digital, a vast array of information on leading is available to anyone who searches for it. This can be bewildering, making it hard to discern what's truly essential.

The first Primary Responsibility in our model reverses some of the negative effects of the rise of management science, which focuses on rational problem-solving and decision-making. As defined in this chapter, Lead is the first of three essential components needed to return leadership and management to a people-centered approach.

Chapter 2 Key Takeaways:

- The first Primary Responsibility is Lead, defined as intentionally influencing and enabling people to accomplish a given task.
- Leading is people-centered while not discounting the need for results.
- Each Primary Responsibility of the model involves a measure of intentionality.

Chapter 3
Primary Responsibility #2: Develop

I was conducting some interviews with team members who had dropped off the team of one particular leader. This leader, Chad, was quite charismatic. Articulate. Gifted. Football captain and class president type of guy (indeed, he'd been both in college). The kind of person who could make things happen. Talk about leading the troops into battle—he could do it. A continuous line of people who wanted to work for him had formed over the years. But there was an equally long line of those who had left his team. We wanted to know why. How could a boss be so appealing, while also inspiring one of the highest team turnover rates in the organization?

We talked to former staff, current staff (under condition of anonymity), and Chad himself. Eventually, our probing revealed a common thread: a lack of appreciation and development of his team members. Each new hire brought his or her talents and experiences to the table. Each was eager to contribute. Yet, after a period of time, each began to feel more drained than filled. More used than appreciated. Hard work was rewarded only with more work and long hours, without much thanks in return. And forget about attending conferences or professional development workshops—Chad said there simply wasn't the time or funding to do that.

Several former staff shared similar stories, independently. In short, they all sensed they were on the team to help Chad look good at their expense without getting much in return themselves. They felt their opportunity to grow and mature in their profession was not with this leader. So, they left.

Interestingly, the line of people who wanted to work for Chad continued to form. After all, he was popular, and he knew how to turn on the charm, telling potential hires things like, "I need you on my team!" and "You'd add so much to my team!" Somehow, he kept the gossip mill under control, too; former employees' disappointment-filled tales were dismissed as resulting from their not having the skills or devotion to do what it takes to succeed. And yet, over time, people couldn't help but begin to wonder why Chad's office nearly always had an opening in it—sometimes two or three.

Leaders can't do it all. No matter how talented or gifted or experienced he or she is, no human leader is omniscient or omnipotent. Leaders need the contributions of others to do what they've been tasked with doing—their skills, resources, time, and talent. The Trusted Leader recognizes and embraces this, seeing people as his or her greatest asset.

The interesting thing about those we lead is that they, like us, are always in a process of growth. Each has talents and strengths as well as weaknesses and limitations. They will be less-developed in some areas, and in need of training and honing of skills. They may bring some latent contributions that you, as a leader, can help uncover. Other tendencies or traits may need to be controlled.

The team, the company, the organization, the home—whatever you're leading—is better when everyone grows in capacity, competence, and contribution. As such, it's imperative for the team leader to *lead with a developmental mindset*. Although I'll introduce this concept here, we'll explore it in greater detail in part II. Be ready to find yourself a little vulnerable at this point, because frankly, this is probably the most neglected responsibility of leaders today.

Leading with a developmental mindset means that, at the end of the day, you aren't satisfied just with getting the job done. Accomplishing your given task *is* important. But it's not enough.

Yes, you want those you lead to do what they're supposed to do. You want your bookkeeper to keep the books properly. As a parent you want your son to learn to make his bed. But there's more—and that's because people are more than robots and machines.

Who a person is *right now* is not the same as who he can *become*. What she contributes now is not all she can and will contribute. Humans are dynamic creatures. Growth, development, and change are encoded in our DNA. As such, we leaders do best if we keep a long-term view, asking ourselves this question: *In addition to* accomplishing the task at hand, who can I help develop in the process, and how? In other words, while completing the immediate assignment, how can I spur those I lead to become different and *better* than they are today?

Leaders who intentionally develop those they lead are the ones who bring out the best in their people.

Defining Develop

Let's break down the definition of Develop just like we did Lead. Here's the full definition:

> **Develop = Intentionally strengthening people's capacity to grow and contribute**

Intentionally

We already covered this idea in the definition of Lead. To recap, it refers to both initiating/stepping up in a situation at hand and planning ahead for future situations.

Strengthening

This word implies something exists that can be made stronger or enhanced. Everyone brings some strength (or multiple strengths) to the table. People will make their greatest contributions in those areas. Their areas of struggle need to be shored up; however, it's generally better to let each person focus on what they are already good at, taking their strengths to an even higher level. This results in a higher-performing team overall, rather than spending a lot of time focusing on getting everyone to a "median" level of proficiency in every area. "Let them do most what they do best." Confidence and competence improve for all with this approach.

People

In defining Lead, I emphasized that people are the leader's greatest asset. Here, we emphasize the fact that your team members are not merely employees; they are real human beings, with full lives just like yours. They're more than teammates or followers. More than names on the organizational chart. They are real people with real potential, real dreams, real abilities, and real insecurities and weaknesses. As such, because we're not dealing with machines but people, the opportunity for growth and development is ever-present. Keeping this at the forefront of your mind will, in the end, enhance each individual *as well as* the entire team and its relational environment.

Capacity

This carries the connotation of an amount or measure of actual or potential ability to perform. Most people's capacity is underdeveloped. An analogy is my understanding (or lack thereof) and ability to use my computer. I know that I am probably only using a fraction of what its actual capacity is. However, there's no way for me to learn everything about how it works at once. It's best to increase my capabilities slowly, taking in a few new things here and there. Similarly, with those you lead, you want to help them expand their current capacity—but not to the extent that you use them up and burn them out.

Notice, the stated purpose in our definition is to increase people's capacity, not to produce more. The idea is not to focus primarily on how to get more out of your team members, but to help them grow—to increase, thrive, and mature. Growth is a foundational principle of all of life; it's how we're wired as humans. We're dynamic, not static. We all like to improve ourselves—to understand more fully, to work more creatively, to learn how to do something better than we did it before. Tapping into this desire will positively affect you *and* those you lead.

Contribute

When you help people grow in their capacity, they will naturally begin to contribute in ever greater ways. They'll add value to your team—and the world beyond. Humans share a deep inner desire to make a difference, to know and be known for who we are and what we can do (from both natural and learned talent). There is a sense of both worth and satisfaction when we can contribute. This sense of doing something that matters—of having an impact—motivates us in ways that a process or performance doesn't. As a leader, you need to ensure that those you lead are all able to contribute in the areas and ways to which they're best suited.

Most Neglected Area

Of the three Primary Responsibilities, Develop is the one most missing in leadership today. With trillions of dollars spent each year on leadership development, how can this be?

The first reason is wrong assumptions—that is, assuming development has happened when it hasn't. With the penchant toward education as information assimilation, we frequently assume that training has occurred simply because information has been dispensed. We hold "training seminars." Notebooks (either paper or digital) are handed out. Lectures are given. There may even be interactive exercises on case studies. All have a measure of helpfulness. Yet, despite the tremendous amount of money and other resources spent on leadership development seminars, conferences, and similar offerings, they're not sufficient by themselves.

Materials may have been distributed and information shared. And, to be honest, these sporadic events are the easiest on the company's budget and time. But our model suggests that another approach will pay much higher dividends.

My twin brother, Jerry, had a novel approach to teaching his middle school English classes what educational development was all about. On the first day of class, he would begin each class by teaching them how to juggle. He would say there are three keys to knowing how to juggle. He would then repeat those three keys over and over. He would demonstrate them. He would drill the students on the three keys, again and again. Then he would give them a pop quiz on how to juggle. Every student would score a perfect grade on this first quiz of the year. "Who made a perfect score?" he would ask afterward. Once all their hands were raised, he would walk over to one student and ask him or her if they knew how to juggle before today. When they replied in the negative, he would hand them the three tennis balls he had used to show them how to juggle. He then instructed the student to go up to the front of the classroom and juggle.

Jerry said that 100 percent of the time, the response from the student was a shocked exclamation, "But I don't know how to juggle!" Jerry would ask her what she made on the quiz. He would point out that, contrary to her protestation of not knowing how to juggle, her score indicated that she did in fact know how to juggle.

What was his point? Being developed or educated in something requires more than merely ingesting information and facts, and then regurgitating them back on a test. Imagine a parent who teaches her child to wash her own laundry; what would happen if the child only has a list of instructions and never practices actually doing the laundry? Development in that one house chore wouldn't occur—and if it's a pattern across all household tasks, then that child will find it unusually challenging to adjust to living alone and managing her own household one day.

Development requires time, experience, observation, and feedback. For most companies and organizations, providing training seminars is much simpler and cheaper. It allows them to check off the "leadership development requirement" for the year. It also leads to the (often false) impression that their employees are being developed.

The second reason Develop may be the weakest element is that leaders have not been taught how (or simply do not care) to lead with a developmental mindset. Doing so takes a deeper level of commitment and intentionality. It is far easier (at least in the short run) to tap into people's existing gifts and experience to accomplish a task and then move on to the next task. But while development does sometimes take place in the doing of a task, it doesn't automatically occur. And when a person is not aware of development occurring, the benefit they glean from it will be greatly limited.

Good leaders don't only lead their people well but see to it that development is taking place at the same time, with the goal of helping them grow and contribute. Every worker—or family member, or other type of team member—should be able to point to a measure of development that occurred in himself or herself while working for you. Good development doesn't happen automatically, though; and you can't send a person to a seminar and assume it happens there either. Leading with a developmental mindset will involve intentional thought and planning on your part.

Development vs. Experience

Before going further, a clarification is in order; in a way, it's part of the same discussion above about leaders assuming development has occurred when it hasn't. There is a subtle but important distinction between developing people and giving them opportunities to gain experience. Yet, we've noticed many leaders equate the two. One leader, David, had this perspective toward those on his team. "Look at all they get to do!" he shared with me in response to my question on how he developed those he supervised. But in exit interviews by those leaving his team, a consistent remark was that they felt that all their hard work and long hours were really designed to help David meet his deadlines and to make him look good to his supervisor rather than for them to grow and develop as professionals. They did not feel they were being given authority and freedom to lead and be creative with projects themselves. Instead, it was always crunch time to help David complete his projects. (People were now voicing these feelings with their feet.)

Here's the key: When you're truly developing those you lead, they will feel empowered by an experience rather than used by it. How do you ensure this happens? Well, we'll get to that in part II.

Chapter 3 Key Takeaways:

- Leading with a developmental mindset means focusing not only on completing the immediate assignment but on spurring those you lead to become better than they are today. This is how you bring out the best in people in the long run.
- Develop, the second Primary Responsibility, is defined as intentionally strengthening your people's capacity to grow and contribute.
- Develop is the most neglected area of leadership today. Reasons include wrong assumptions and a lack of understanding of how to develop others.

Chapter 4
Primary Responsibility #3: Care

I was out in the driveway shooting some baskets as my wife, Sherry, about eight months pregnant with our fourth child at the time, was sitting on a bench off to the side. We were casually chatting between shots when she suddenly pronounced, "I don't feel like you're taking good care of me."

"Wow, where did that come from?" I thought. But I knew the answer: she was speaking from her heart. And I could see in her expression that she was taking a chance by being both honest and vulnerable with me. Briefly tempted to keeping shooting, I knew this was no talk to have between baskets. So, I tucked the ball under my arm and went over and sat down beside her.

"Why do you feel that way?" I asked, genuinely perplexed.

"You're just so busy all the time, always on the go. I feel like I'm watching you sprint through life while I'm walking, which makes us feel out of sync with each other. Even when you're not working, it feels like we can't just relax and enjoy being together like we used to do, many years ago. I miss that—just being together, and knowing you care about what I'm feeling and thinking. I don't want to feel like I'm watching you do life, as an observer; I don't want to feel overlooked amidst all your productivity and action."

I kept quiet as she shared, fighting internal defenses as they ran through my mind. When she finished, she looked at me and waited. Rarely at a loss for words, I didn't know what to say. After a couple moments of silence, I finally spoke my heart back.

"I love you, Sherry; you know that," I said. "I work hard, provide a good living, spend as much time as I possibly can with you. And compared to a lot of other husbands, I think I do pretty well in taking care of you and the kids. But it's obvious I'm not doing as well as I thought. It's hard to hear this. Help me understand how I can do better."

Now, don't worry, my wife and I are doing well; but like every couple, we have moments of difference and miscommunication—times when we need to clear up wrong assumptions and express our concerns to each other. This particular conversation was illuminating and a turning point for me as I owned up to my struggle in the area of Care.

The old saying that people "don't care how much you know until they know how much you care" may be a cliché, but it is true nonetheless. And care is best seen from the perspective of the one being cared for rather than the one caring. This is evident from the basketball scenario.

I really love and care about my wife. My desire for her to feel cared for is sincere. But notice how she stated her declaration: "I don't *feel like* you're taking good care of me." Care is sensed first at the feelings level. What is said doesn't count as much as what is experienced. Telling my wife that I thought she was mistaken was not the approach to follow in this situation, nor would it have helped allay her feelings—in fact, it'd likely have made her feel worse. I was obviously falling short of *her* definition of being cared for, and her definition mattered.[8] As I listened to her, it became apparent to me that, in my busyness with work, I had been falling short in how I showed care for my wife. This was hard to hear. But it was what I *needed* to hear. And soon I adjusted my actions to address my wife's concern.

Defining Care

> Care = Intentionally watching over and responding to people's needs and well-being.

Intentionally

This word appears a third time. This is because none of the three Primary Responsibilities of leadership happens on their own. We have to make them happen. They need to be at the forefront of our thinking and actions. When it comes to caring, intentionality is especially important in a business setting. In a bottom line–driven, profits-focused

---

8 It's possible that a person can have unreasonable expectations or feelings that are off-base from reality; thus, you can take this too far. But as a leader, and as a person in general, it's always best to assume one may have a blind spot and to take the other person's feelings and perspective into consideration.

world, it can be easy to get carried away with tasks and productivity and forget to care for those we lead *as human beings*. They aren't there to be used, like objects or machines. They are real people with real feelings and lives.

Watching Over

This phrase carries the notion of seeing. Do we see what we need to see? Or are we seeing only what we *want* to see? Are we aware of what is right before us? For many leaders, and it seems this is especially the case for male leaders, seeing our leadership landscape for what it is— and not only for what we want to see—is more difficult than we often realize. In general, leaders tend to focus more on the big picture than the details, so we can often miss what is in plain sight.

I asked one dad how things were going in his life, and his response was, "Well, no one's crying at the moment, so I guess everything is fine." We tend to notice what's big and loud while we may miss the subtler things about a situation. What are others communicating by their eyes, the tones of their voices, their facial expressions, or their silence? This is the social awareness component of emotional intelligence. Are you picking up on the cues those you lead are sending to you—both the obvious ones and the subtler ones?

Responding

It's one thing to see or observe; it's another thing to *respond*. This is the idea of moving toward something—taking some action visible to others. It is going beyond intent and good motives. We often think people see our intentions, but more often, they only see our actions or lack thereof. This was the case with Sherry and me. And this can be the case with our kids. How many young athletes cast a searching and often disappointed eye into the stands hoping that their dad will at last show up for a game, as he said he would?

Needs

To what should the leader be responding? In the context of our definition, the leader should be responding to the needs of those he or she is leading.

Needs refer to a condition marked by the lack of something requisite. The range of a person's needs is almost limitless, from a word of encouragement to a missing skill to a kick in the pants. When we speak of responding to needs as a leader, we obviously don't mean that you can or should meet *every* human need that those you lead have. That would not only be impossible but inappropriate. There are boundaries within your realm of authority, and as a boss, you're not there to meet your team members' personal need for self-esteem boosts and the like.

In an office setting, some areas of need within your purview may include the following:

- The need to be noticed
- The need to be acknowledged for effort and work
- The need to be appreciated and valued
- The need for feedback
- The need to be taken seriously
- The need for help
- The need to voice their thoughts and ideas (and to be heard)
- The need to make a contribution

Well-Being

While needs are more about the details of each person and team, well-being speaks to the overall atmosphere of an office or team. This refers to the team's collective state of health, happiness, and prosperity. Are team members generally in a good and satisfactory condition of existence? Is anything significantly wrong with one of them that is affecting everyone else, or is there a problem relationally between two or more of them?

To evaluate well-being, ask questions such as:

- What is the tone of the team members when they're together?
- What is the atmosphere in the office on a daily basis?

Most of us have been in extremely tense situations. That kind of atmosphere hanging in the air on a regular basis is not healthy or beneficial for anyone. Patrick Lencioni speaks to this idea of well-being in his best-seller *The Advantage*. A key point of the book is that the culture of the team is critically important and has tremendous impact on everyone. The work or team environment can range from toxic to healthy, with strong team satisfaction, communication, and cooperation.

Observing a company's executive team often provides a window into the well-being of the organization as a whole. This was certainly the case with one company my colleagues and I helped a few years ago. This entity had been experiencing significant employee turnover, and we were asked to come in and help identify the cause and possible solutions. The company was a good one overall, with a great niche in its industry. Still, employees kept leaving. To start, I asked if I could sit in on an executive team meeting. Within minutes of watching, I observed two problems. For one, the leaders were very guarded and cautious while speaking, keeping their cards close to the vest. From some pre-meeting conversations with team members, I knew they had a lot to say about the upcoming agenda, but for some reason they weren't voicing those ideas in the group meeting. Secondly, when team members addressed each other, their comments seemed to carry a subtle barb. While not outwardly belligerent, their reactions and tone went beyond the ideological level—tensions lay unspoken beneath the surface. If this executive team's well-being represented the whole organization, I knew we had our work cut out for us.

Fortunately, when I honestly explained our concerns, the executive team was receptive and agreed to work on the overall well-being of the company. After we helped this team for a couple of years (corporate culture does take time to change!), the progress was discernable. The board chair even announced to the executive team that he was very encouraged with the quality of leaders the company now had in place and with the goodwill he saw among those leaders. Unsurprisingly, the turnover rate dropped drastically in that time.

Also a Neglected Area

Care is the most *felt* neglected area in leadership. In his book *Leaders Eat Last*, Simon Sinek states that "when a leader embraces their responsibility to care for people instead of caring for numbers, then people will follow, solve problems and see to it that that leader's vision comes to life the right way, a stable way and not the expedient way." Interestingly, I have never met a leader who said he or she didn't care for those he or she led.

In fact, leaders usually go through a litany of the personal sacrifices they are making for those they lead. And they really mean it. Yet, so often, the followers feel otherwise. Why the discrepancy?

It's difficult to translate what's in one's heart and mind into actions that resonate with another's heart and mind. Everyone has an intuitive sense that they're cared for (or not). But the way this intuition is sensed differs from person to person, just as the possible expressions of care are nearly endless. (When speaking of a family or other type of personal relationship, one author refers to these differing expressions of care as "love languages."[9]) For some, a card saying, "Thinking of You," speaks care; for another, he feels cared for when his leader remembers to ask about his sick mother.

Our tendency is to assume a certain manifestation of care will suffice for everyone, but this is not necessarily the case. Taking time to understand those we lead, and to translate our care and empathy into their "language" will help them know we value them as humans (for who they are), not just as workers (for what they do for us).

I stated this earlier, but it bears repeating: Those we lead are real people. They have dreams and aspirations. Fears and insecurities. They have contributions they long to make. They have tendencies they try to hide. They have relational dynamics taking place not only in the workplace but outside it as well. Many have financial pressures that confront them. Still, they are the leader's greatest asset and should be treated as such. No matter if you're a warm, loving type of personality naturally or someone who struggles to show others your care and concern, without this third Primary Responsibility, your leadership will be incomplete and diminished. All three—Lead, Develop, and Care—truly are critical.

Chapter 4 Key Takeaways:

- Care, the third and final Primary Responsibility, is defined as intentionally watching over and responding to the needs and well-being of your people.

---

9   The author is Gary Chapman, whose five love languages described in his book of the same title include acts of service, words of affirmation, receiving gifts, quality time, and physical touch. These relate more to a spousal relationship or friendship, but his concept that people sense others' care in different ways is broadly applicable.

- While Develop is the most neglected area of leadership today, Care is the area that people who are led *feel* leaders most neglect.
- Caring for those we lead does not have a one-size-fits-all approach or method because people are all different.

Before Continuing to Part II

Now that we've fully defined each component of our model, you're beginning to see the common threads and the way all the parts work together. No doubt, you're itching to know how to put some of these ideas into practice. We'll get there soon enough, but before moving on, I encourage you to take a moment for personal leadership assessment:

1. Have you identified your strength, stretch, and struggle area of Lead, Develop, and Care (using our definitions)? If so, what are they? If you're still unsure, ask a colleague or friend (someone who knows you well) to help you out. Remember, there is no right or wrong answer—just your answer. It's important to be as honest as possible in answering. Resist the common temptation to fill in your answers based on the way you want to be viewed.
2. Think about your strength area: In what ways do you think you could enhance or develop this area even more? You will make your greatest contribution in your area of strength. But remember, even though this area is already stronger and more natural for you, it still needs ongoing development.
3. Now let's turn to your struggle area: In what ways do you think this weakness has hurt your team (or one or more of its members)? This isn't a time to beat yourself up but to take honest stock of your leadership. Don't be afraid to look your weaknesses square in the face. And have no fear! We're not stranding you, because as you continue to read, parts II and III will enable you to walk away with some concrete ideas for how to improve.

Part II
The Operational Aspects

I could tell why Elissa's company designated her as a regional director. She was intelligent, articulate, highly capable, experienced in leading others. But I'd been tasked with providing training for her and her fellow regional directors, so I needed to probe into what exactly a regional director did—how they each understood and carried out their roles on a day-to-day basis.

To that end, I asked Elissa, "Apart from the usual scheduling of meetings, managing production quotas and deadlines, responding to interoffice communication, and addressing obstacles as they surface, what do you actually do as a regional leader?"

She started to answer but hesitated. She finally asked, "Do you mean what is my job description?"

"Not exactly," I responded. "I think I have a fairly clear understanding of the things for which you are responsible on paper. My question is more along the lines of, 'How do you go about leading in those responsibilities?'"

Her articulation faltered as she fumbled for an answer. "I, uh, um, well, you know. I just lead."

"No, I really don't know," I said. "Could you help me understand?"

Knowing about a concept is one thing. Knowing how to put it into practice is quite another thing. The former does not guarantee the latter. In fact, we have seen that familiarity with a term or concept often lulls us into a false sense of understanding and competency that we have neither thought through adequately nor practiced effectively.

As we were developing our model, we knew we needed more than the Primary Responsibilities. Those three words make the model memorable. They bring clarity amidst complexity. But leaders also need to know how to put those concepts into operation. Based on our research and decades of experience both leading and developing leaders, we settled on twelve Operational Aspects: four for each Primary Responsibility. Dozens more could have been chosen, but we wanted to keep the model as uncluttered as possible—stick to the essentials.

The Operational Aspects explored in part II may not necessarily be new to you. But don't let familiar terms lull you to sleep! In a sense, we hope you will begin to see how familiar concepts fit together under the larger umbrellas we've already established (Lead, Develop, and Care).

Here are the Operational Aspects for each Primary Responsibility. We'll devote one chapter for each.

Chapter 5
Lead Operational Aspect #1:
Set Direction

Entering the coffee shop, I spied my new client across the room and went to join him at the table he'd claimed. This was my first time meeting Barry, the middle manager of a company focused on developing young leaders in South Carolina.

After the initial pleasantries and introductions, I got right to it: "Barry, share with me about your work. What's it all about?"

Enthusiastically, and with a clear sense of satisfaction, he proceeded to pull up his calendar of events for the young leaders on his tablet. As he talked, I scanned the list: Social mixer with local CEOs. Field trip to the Capitol. Skills development workshops aplenty. Internship and job fairs, mock interviews, and even a weekend retreat. And that was just the next few months! He certainly had a lot going on.

Before I could say anything in response, Barry leaned forward and lowered his voice. "And guess what?" he said, brimming with pride. "I've got a connection at the White House who thinks they can get us in to meet the president! The kids will be stoked … well, at least some of them will," he added with a laugh.

"Wow! All that sounds great!" I said, pausing before I went on. "Can I ask you a question, Barry?" He waved at me to continue. Shifting into a more serious tone, I told him that I could see he was very busy. He nodded. "But," I asked, "where are you going with all these activities? What's the overarching goal or goals you're trying to accomplish through them?"

As Barry searched for a response, I clarified further: "What kind of leaders do you want to produce as a result of your organization, and how are these activities achieving that?"

To my surprise, Barry admitted that he hadn't really thought about these questions very much; he was just doing the things he knew his organization was expected to do. He was like that proverbial pilot—lost but making great time.

As I talked with the rest of his leadership team, they each confessed to me, separately, that while they were all extremely busy, they felt directionless beyond their daily routine. They had fallen into the common pattern of planning activities "just because we have always done them," while losing sight of the target goal of those activities. Burnout was on the horizon, if not already here, for several of them. My client needed to act soon—for everyone's sake.

Setting direction is all about having a target. Where are you going? What are you trying to accomplish? What's the purpose for all of your actions?

When I look around at leaders in their homes, their work environments, or their community engagements, there's no lack of activity. Everyone is busy. Everyone is making great time at something. But is this activity producing its intended outcome? Are these leaders, and those they lead, going anywhere in particular?

Leaders must take time to think out and plan the direction of the enterprise they lead. They must steer in a certain direction—or risk getting everyone lost, confused, and disillusioned. The direction in which to go may not be obvious, so it demands careful thought; it requires resisting the temptation to be shortsighted (as all humans are tempted toward) and to consider the long term. It means not succumbing to the inertia of the moment, the tyranny of the urgent. And it's crucial to leadership, because without setting direction, a leader ends up just managing everyone's busyness.

More Than Naming a Target

Setting direction is about having a target, but it's not only about naming that target; it's about having a clear plan for reaching it.

My favorite college football team is the University of Alabama. My family and I lived in the state in the 1970s, my oldest daughter was born in Tuscaloosa, and we developed friendships with a number of the players while we lived there. Whether you share my love for the Crimson Tide or you hate them, there's no denying that Nick Saban has been very successful in his tenure as Alabama's head coach.

What direction do you think Coach Saban sets each year for his team? The answer is obvious: to win the national championship. In fact, every college sports coach has that as his target, or at least his dream. Yet, few coaches have the system in place that can actually get them there—more than once.

Naming the ultimate target is necessary, but it's only the start to setting direction. An organization's mission or purpose statement may be the target—and knowing it is important—but you need more. A mission statement merely indicates which game you're playing. It does not necessarily tell you where you are in the game right now or how to proceed.

Just as college football hasn't seen many coaches like Nick Saban, the leadership arena includes many who struggle in this area of setting direction. Frankly, it's one of the harder components of Lead to do well.

In some situations, setting direction may be more straightforward. For example, a project manager needs to develop a product (the target) by a specified deadline within a given budget with a certain team. Yet, if you add the element of developing team members *while* completing the product, the project takes on a different dimension. The project—like any undertaking—presents the opportunity to do more than merely finishing the task at hand.

College professors are the leaders of their classrooms. I had some outstanding ones. And then there were those whose qualification to teach at that level was questioned by the entire class. In those latter cases, the issue was rarely a lack of command of the subject matter (that's obviously important). What made the real difference between the good professors and the bad professors was whether they had the ability to bring us along with them as they lectured. Our brains have a built-in need for clarity in direction. We're looking for the hooks on which to hang the ideas we're hearing. Some of the instructors would begin presenting ideas as if they had simply opened a page in the middle of the dictionary and started reading. We simply could not follow and understand where they were going with their talks. The best and easiest teachers to learn from were the ones who took time to introduce the lecture with both a statement of the target and a clear outline of how they planned to arrive there. Here's an example:

> Sets Direction: "Today we are going to talk about the four main causes of the First World War. These were militarism, alliances, imperialism, and nationalism. Let's begin with militarism … "

> Fails to Set Direction: "In the early 1900s, the German Empire announced its intention to create a navy as big as Britain's. An arms race began shortly thereafter."

Notice, the second statement above isn't necessarily unclear, and it's possible students will eventually begin to see where the professor is headed. But the failure to set the stage or lay out a roadmap for the lecture creates confusion, and unless the professor himself has a clear outline toward the target lesson, students are likely to remain in a sea of facts with no overarching understanding of the topic.

Getting Past the Superficial and the Ambiguous

It takes substantial time and effort to set direction well. I once was coaching a business team in Montevideo, Uruguay. I gave the team members a worksheet with six questions on it, to which they had to respond according to their unique leadership situation. Each question was concerned with setting direction (and is now encoded in our Set Direction Tool, described below in detail and also found in part III). As we were starting, one of the leaders, Mateo, commented that he and his team had just completed an exercise along these same lines. I said, "Oh, good, then this should be easy for you to do."

When they had completed the assignment, I asked Mateo if I could walk through the questions with him, with his teammates listening. He agreed and eagerly began reading his answers aloud one at a time. Periodically, I would ask him to stop so I could probe deeper with some additional questions to help us understand his thinking.

Two and a half hours later, we finished the sixth question. An exercise that Mateo thought would take five minutes to go over took far longer than he expected—and his assumption was typical among others who have completed this tool. By the end, Mateo put his hand on his forehead and quipped, "Oh my goodness. I never realized how superficial we were in setting direction. I never realized there was so much more to this. I can see why we aren't getting the results we're after. We've been way too general and ambiguous."

Mateo and his team members' approach to setting direction had been sort of like Nick Saban spending five minutes telling his players on the first day of practice that the target for the year was to win the national championship—and leaving it at that.

To set direction well, you have to do much more than share the final goal. You need to offer more concrete steps for getting there.

How to Set Direction

Our Set Direction Tool in part III uses six questions to help you break through the usual superficiality of this Operational Aspect. These questions are as follows:

1. Who should be setting direction?
2. Where are we going?
3. Why are we going there?
4. What does success look like?
5. What are our current realities?
6. Which boundaries do we need to get there?

Let's briefly go over what these questions are about and why they're important so you can make good use of this tool.

Question 1: Who should be setting direction?

Every leadership situation is different. For example, if Mom and Dad are planning the family's summer vacation, they probably won't enlist two-year-old Johnny to aid in the planning process. However, if the kids are much older, their participation may become integral. As leader, you're ultimately responsible for setting direction, but you may enlist others to help in that process. To determine the "who," ask yourself:

- Is this a situation where *I* alone (or I along with my boss) should determine the direction, and then *inform* my team?
- Should I determine the direction but then *solicit feedback from the team* before setting it finally?
- Should the *team together* determine the direction (in a more democratic process)?

There's not one way to set direction. That being said, it's advisable with adults and team members to allow those who are responsible for carrying out the direction to have some input in setting the direction. The overall direction (whether it's winning the national championship or becoming the top producer of widgets in your state) may come down from on high, but processing these questions together with your team will add depth, detail, and buy-in. (It will also help you see where there may be misunderstandings or wrong assumptions.)

Question 2: Where are we going?

Assumptions can easily take over with respect to the "where" question. You're part of a large company whose mission statement is proudly displayed on a plaque in the foyer. Everyone knows the target goal…or do they? Do they remember it? Do they understand *how* you're reaching it?

For years I was the national director of a large organization with chapters in every U.S. state. As I would visit the various chapters, I would pull the team together and ask, "Now, what are we trying to do here?" Often, the response was, "Well, isn't that obvious?" I'd reply, "Great, then it will be easily articulated. How would you state it?" Oftentimes, the team members soon ran out of vocabulary. It wasn't so much that they didn't know their goal, but in the midst of the busyness of work, they had forgotten the goal. We tend to look only at the small section of the path before us. Every now and then, we need to look up and remember the long view.

It's been said that if there is a mist at the top, there's a fog down below. If the leaders are cloudy on where they are going (or at least on how to communicate it), the sense of direction only gets foggier the further down the line you go.

Where are you going with your family? In your marriage? With your team at work? To get at these answers, you can ask some more questions, such as, Where do I *want* to go? Where do I *need* to go? or What values, behaviors, responses, skills, traditions, or memories do I want to move toward?

For example, if you have children, what values do you want to see them develop? Learning to treat people with dignity and respect has to be taught (and modeled); it's not just caught. At work, besides finishing the project at hand, what skills would you want to see your direct reports develop in the process of completing the project?

Question 3: Why are we going there?

This question is about whether the direction you're headed is compelling. In other words, is it worth the time and effort? One group I helped in Europe launched a very ambitious initiative that would require every ounce of energy and resources they had for it to succeed. In talking to the top leadership, this initiative was the focus of practically every conversation. As an exercise, I gave each of the executive team's eight members a 3-inch-by-5-inch card and asked them to write down two reasons why they were doing this initiative. They had four minutes to do it.

When the time was up, I went around the room and asked each person to share one of the two reasons they wrote down and continued around the room until all the reasons were voiced. Then I asked, "Would any of those reasons get you out of bed in the morning? That is, would any of the reasons you just stated be compelling enough to motivate you to make it happen?" They sat there for a moment, and then one of them sighed, shook his head, and said, "Not very compelling, were they?" I had to say to them that they faced a daunting reality. Three hundred of their staff would be arriving the following day. This team's task was to launch this initiative, and yet they were both unclear as to the difference this initiative would make and unconvinced of its worth. It sounded good and noble. It even had a catchy title. But they had not really plumbed the depths of the *why* question.

This question is not about firing up people like a cheerleader. Often a pep talk is more like a sugar high—it makes an immediate impression but then burns out quickly. This element is really about clarity of worth and value. With all the things competing for our time, attention, effort, and resources, is *this* direction worth the focus? Will it produce what you need it to produce?

Question 4: What does success look like?

What is success? What's the win? How do we know we've accomplished what we set out to do? This question often goes unanswered. If the target is raising a set amount of money in a capital campaign, the goal is clear, and progress is easily measured and demonstrated. However, more often than not, the target sounds much more generic—and one will hardly know when one has achieved success. One job description for an administrative assistant reads, "Serve the department head by providing prompt and effective administrative help." While a good start, this description is far too generic—how will the person in this position know what success is? What does prompt and effective help look like, more specifically?

Likewise, a religious organization might have a lofty goal to "encourage spiritual growth among its members"; but how do you know when this has been done successfully? What specifically will occur that will let you know you've accomplished (or are in the process of accomplishing) what you've set out to do?

Those to whom you, as a leader, assign a responsibility cannot read your mind. As a leader, you may have specific expectations concerning outcomes, but it's unfair to assume that these outcomes are understood by those who serve you if you never communicate them. You must get these outcomes out of your mind and into the minds of those who will help realize them. Ask yourself, "What would this look like when it's done well?" Then articulate this vision to those you lead, engaging in a dialogue until you come to a mutual understanding of what success or accomplishment of the task should look like.

Question 5: What are our current realities?

Where do we find ourselves as an organization (or as a family/group)? What's different from when we started out together? A keyword that helps with this question is to add the adverb "now": What are our current realities *now*?

I enjoy playing golf. As I stand on the tee box, I can see that the direction I'm shooting for is the flag stick on the green in the far distance. It is both obvious and clear. My direction is the flag stick.

However, I don't hit all my shots as straight as I'd like. I often find myself off to the side of the fairway instead of in the middle of it. In fact, let's say that after my initial tee shot, again aiming for the green, I pull my shot and end up behind a large tree in the rough. As I step around the tree, I can still see the flag stick on the green. The overall direction of where I'm heading is still clear. Yet, the tree is completely blocking any shot toward the green.

Now, I have many clubs in my golf bag. Yet, I don't have any clubs that will enable me to hit the ball through the trunk of a tree. I could cut the tree down, but I'm fairly confident the club managers would do more than frown on that action. So, what do I have to do given my current reality? I can't keep going in the same direction I started. Instead, I have to change my direction by chipping to the side rather than forward to get me back into play. The current situation required a temporary shift in direction.

One European leader, Liesel, sat at a table unable to write much in response to these six questions. "You seem stuck," I commented. She nodded and explained that the direction her team was going had been accomplished—namely, the government in her country had given her permission to start an aid program for abused women. To her, she had reached the flag stick and the ball was in the cup, but she wasn't sure where the next hole was—to continue with the golfing metaphor.

I asked Liesel another question: "Do you have a team to help you with this work?"

"Yes, five other women," she replied.

"Good," I replied. "Now are these women competent and confident to meet the needs of those they will be trying to help?"

"Oh, not to the point that they need to be," she replied.

"What does that current reality require in terms of a new direction for you?"

She caught on quickly, responding, "Getting them trained and ready for the service we want to provide."

"Right," I said. "You now have a new target that requires your leadership!"

Question 6: Which boundaries do we need to get there?

Henry Cloud, in his book *Boundaries for Leaders*, points out that it's not enough to define the destination of where you're going. One must also look at what will get you there. As Cloud explains, one must set (and maintain) boundaries:

> A "boundary" is a property line. It defines where your property begins and ends. If you think about your home, on your property, you can define what is going to happen there, and what is not. You are "ridiculously in charge"…[These boundaries] are guardrails that make sure certain things happen, prevent other things from happening, and keep it all moving forward.[10]

Thus, this sixth and final question asks the question, "What drives success?"

Dr. Howard Hendricks once said, "The secret of concentration is elimination."[11] The direction can be clear, compelling, and agreed-upon but still missed because of the inability to define the few must-do essentials that will get you there *and/or* the inability to limit the things that will not get you there.

I initiated a one-year staff development program for university graduates who were joining our organization. To develop the curriculum for the program, I pulled together a handful of experienced staff developers. The question before us was, "What content does this curriculum need to contain to enable these young hires to be successful at what we're asking them to do?"

The brainstorming began, and I began to record as much of the discussion as possible on a flipchart. Pretty soon, we had filled ten pages, which I taped to the walls so these trainers could see all the things they had named as absolutely essential for these graduates to receive. They were still not finished, but I finally put up my hand and stopped them. "Hold

---

10 Henry Cloud, *Boundaries for Leaders: Results, Relationships, and Being Ridiculously in Charge* (New York: Harper Business, 2013), 14–15, 17.

11 www.azquotes.com/quote/608849.

it!" I said. "This is crazy. It will take ten years for them to get all this stuff! This is a one-year internship. Realistically, what *four or five* things can and should we train them in during the twelve months we have them? We have to focus on those few things and eliminate all the other items."

The developers were not easily persuaded. To them, every topic was important. I emphasized again that the issue wasn't whether all of these elements were important or not; the issue was whether they were important *right now* for the success of the new staff.

In our desire to be comprehensive, we can actually set up those we lead for failure. It is imperative as leaders that we give thought and attention to what we will *not* do in addition to what we *must* do. Steve Jobs at Apple is well known for saying that he was as proud of what Apple didn't make as for what the company did make … and the success of his mindset speaks for itself!

———————

To conclude, setting direction requires far more work than we often think is necessary. But the effort is essential and well worthwhile. Patrick Lencioni summarizes the outcome that will ensue: "Members of the leadership team know, agree on, and are passionate about the reason that the organization exists. The leadership team has a clear, current goal around which they rally. They feel a collective sense of ownership for that goal."[12] What leader doesn't want to lead a team like that?

Chapter 5 Key Takeaways:

- Setting direction—steering a team toward a particular goal or target—is essential or else a leader will just end up managing everyone's busyness.
- Setting direction means not only having a target but a clear plan to achieve it.
- Six questions in the Set Direction Tool (see part III) help you nail down direction: where you are going, why and how, and what it looks like when you get there.

---

12 Patrick Lencioni, *The Advantage: Why Organizational Health Trumps Everything Else in Business* (San Francisco: Jossey-Bass, 2012), 196.

Chapter 6
Lead Operational Aspect #2: Align

Debbie—leader of an interdisciplinary team of health-care professionals at a local hospital—was encouraged that her team had agreed on the general direction to head. There had been some lively, emotion-laden debate in the process. Because of her temperament, this was a heavy burden on Debbie; she really disliked heated discussions and was relieved when the vote was finally taken—especially since her view had won the majority.

With the direction decided, she was glad to be moving on, and she assumed everyone else would jump on board now too.

It was a wrong—and costly—assumption.

In subsequent days, Debbie noticed that the team seemed to be facing some strong headwinds and progress was slow. She also noticed that the three who had been the most vocal in the minority position of the debate on direction appeared to be somewhat disengaged from moving forward. The trio were present at team meetings but quiet and aloof. They didn't seem to be bringing their best contributions to the discussions. They often ate lunch together in their own little cluster with hushed conversation.

Debbie finally confronted these three. In reply, they explained that they had not voted for the direction the team was now heading, still felt it was the wrong one, and were convinced the plan would not succeed. Debbie knew that as their supervisor, she had the authority and power to make them do the work. She also realized, however, that she wanted more than tacit agreement. She wanted and needed their alignment with the direction they were heading. She was unsure what to do now that she saw that setting direction hadn't automatically brought everyone on board with that direction.

Once you've set direction—you know where you're going—the next Operational Aspect is Align: get everyone and every aspect of your team (or family or group) moving in the same direction so that you can, together, achieve the results you desire. Without alignment, the proverbial "herding cats" syndrome takes hold; everyone might still be moving, but not necessarily all in the same direction!

Aligning is about *bringing together*. It does not mean everyone is suddenly thinking and doing the exact same thing. Think of an American football team, as an example; on any given play, eleven players on offense are all committed to the same play (designed to move the ball down the field and ultimately score), but each player is performing a different function to contribute to the success of the play. They are unified in the direction of the play but diversified in its execution. Most teams in any setting work in a similar way.

The question is, how do you align well? How do you bring together those you're leading to move in the direction you've set? In particular, what are the areas that need alignment? Henry Cloud, in his book *Boundaries for Leaders*, suggests three key areas: thinking, actions, and resources. Cloud includes human resources in the third area, but I have broken out people into its own category in my discussion below.

Thinking

Thinking is multifaceted, involving the content of thoughts about your direction as well as a deeper understanding of that direction, the larger perspective, and attitudes toward the direction.

Everything stems from our thinking: Our behaviors, practices, and reactions all flow from our values and motives, which find their genesis in what we think and believe. To get your team demonstrating the same actions requires some time focusing on their thinking. You can all sit around the same table engaged in the same discussion, but because you each process that discussion differently, you may each come to very different conclusions. As Henry Cloud says, "The prevailing thinking patterns of a team or organization—its norms and belief systems—will define what it is and what it does."[13]

---

13 Cloud, *Boundaries for Leaders*, 101.

To continue with the American football illustration, in an offensive team huddle, an alignment of thinking takes place. The players gather closely together to hear the quarterback call the play. His calling of the next play orients the other ten players' thinking toward the same plan—and based on prior training and practice, each should then know what his role is in that play.

How many times have you said or heard others say, "Oh, I thought we were … "? This kind of remark is a clear indication that his or her thinking was not in alignment with others' thinking. If the receivers think the quarterback called a running play when he actually called a pass play, the play would not succeed. Thus, alignment must involve thinking together toward the same plan of action.

But alignment of thinking is about more than just content of thought. It requires a common understanding, perspective, and general attitude.

Understanding

Closely tied to thinking is understanding, referring to knowledge of and familiarity with something. It's vital that every "player" on your team understands the "play" (or set of plays) called in order to proceed in the determined direction, along with the role he or she is supposed to carry out. In other words, there needs to be universal agreement among team members about what the next step is toward the direction you're headed, and what is expected of each of them. Achieving this agreement will require a level of specificity by you as the leader—something that is too often assumed or left in overly vague terms.

Here are three sets of questions to ask your team (in a group setting) to aid your alignment in understanding:

1. Could someone express what you understand to be the task/decision before us right now?
   Follow-up questions: Is that how everyone else understands it? Who sees it differently?
2. What do you understand your specific role to be based on this understanding? That is, what is expected of you?
   Have everyone go around and state their roles briefly if it's a small enough number of people—or, for larger groups, have them write their understanding down for now, and then you

as a leader can communicate the roles in a summary fashion now or later.

3. What have we concluded or agreed upon?
    Follow-up question: Is everyone in agreement with this understanding of our conclusion(s)?

Have someone restate the decision/task. Then, invite anyone to speak up now or to talk to you later if they disagree. With this final question, for some key decisions (especially involving personnel, major financial expenditures, or changes in direction for the company), it's helpful to give the team time to let the decision "percolate"—consider it as being in "wet cement" for twenty-four hours. This is important since people process ideas at different speeds, and a momentary pause in the finalization of the agreement can help avoid a bad or incomplete decision. The main purpose is be open to the question, "Did we miss anything?" This is not the opportunity for the team members in the minority on the vote to mount a renewed argument of their position. Rather, it's a time to see if anything new needs to be considered before the decision is officially set and announced.

Perspective

Perspective means seeing all the relevant data in meaningful relationship. Nothing happens in a vacuum. Our thinking and understanding need to be related to the current circumstances—the larger picture or environment.

In the football analogy, when a team is behind in the score with only two minutes left in the game, it's important that players' perspectives are aligned—they need a joint sense of urgency and a common understanding of how the team is to function in *this* situation.

Asking these three questions can help with alignment of perspective:

1. What are the circumstances facing us?
2. Where are we receiving pressure from without? … from within?
3. Have we thoroughly considered the perspectives of age, gender, ethnicity, competition, costs, benefits, and any other relevant factors?

I was teaching one of our leadership symposiums in Vienna, Austria. I began to notice that for many of the Austrians, especially many of the men, there was a subtle but discernable hesitancy about the very concept of leadership. I was puzzled by it.

On the afternoon of the second day, one of our Viennese hosts was giving us a brief tour of the central part of the city. When we came to a large stone memorial, written in German, our host shared that this was where the dreaded Gestapo were headquartered in Vienna during the Second World War. The memorial was a tribute to all who lost their lives under the Nazi tyranny. It was then that the light bulb went on as our host explained that the German word for leader is *führer*; as a title, though, it's often associated with Hitler, explaining the Austrians' resistance to the idea of being leaders. The concept of a leader has always been a positive one (overall) to me, but I now understood why the Austrians' perspective of leadership was so different from mine. The very mention of the term "leader" was an automatic reminder of a dark chapter in their nation's existence. Understanding this enabled us to shift our approach in helping them.

Attitudes

"Attitude is a little thing that makes a big difference."[14] Attitudes out of alignment can kill direction—and success. Patrick Lencioni speaks to this problem in *The Five Dysfunctions of a Team*. In this classic book, he describes the dysfunction of artificial harmony, which can be even more toxic than open disagreement among team members.[15] On the surface, there may be agreement. This was the case with Debbie's team, from the opening vignette. But the private conversations that followed told a different tale. Continued, silent disagreement with the final decision on direction by three people was accompanied by a spirit of sulky dissatisfaction and disengagement. The presence of such an attitude casts doubt over the ultimate success of the project.

Accomplishment of any goal can be difficult given the many hurdles and obstacles that crop up along the way (some foreseeable, some not). It is even more difficult when some on the team have a bad attitude

---

14 This quote has been misattributed to various people ranging from Winston Churchill to Zig Ziglar; its actual source is unknown.

15 Patrick Lencioni, *The Five Dysfunctions of a Team: A Leadership Fable* (San Francisco: Jossey-Bass, 2002), 92.

toward the goal. These people simply will not give themselves whole-heartedly to the success of the direction you've set—which spells trouble for everyone.

Asking *yourself* these questions can help with attitude alignment individually:

1. Where do you find negativity thinking? (This is not the same as thinking critically or realistically. Negativity thinking starts with the conclusion that "it won't work," no matter what; it's a killer for creativity and proactivity.)
2. Where is there "learned helplessness?" (A concept that has appeared in the management literature for some time, this is the idea that things are going badly, will always go badly, and there is nothing that can be done to counter this pattern. This attitude, too, is a torpedo for progress.)
3. Where are the cliques? (In general, these can be spotted at the coffee breaks—they're the clusters of colleagues that automatically form outside the conference room.)

Asking these questions *of your team* can help with attitude alignment as a group:

1. Now that the decision has been made, in all honesty, what are you feeling toward it?
2. Are you "all in" with this decision/direction that's been established? If not, what's holding you back?
3. On a scale of 1 to 10, how wholeheartedly can you promote and defend this decision?

On the third team question, when there is a low number in response, you as the leader can follow with any of these questions:

- Do you feel you have shared your thoughts adequately, have been understood, listened to, and taken seriously?
- Is there something still missing in your understanding on which you would like more explanation?
- Do you need a bit more time to process the decision?
- As you examine what's driving you, would you say you are trying to help us understand or trying to convince us of your position?

If a minority of team members feel they have been listened to and taken seriously, yet the vote doesn't go the way they desired, it's imperative that you as the leader still make your decision. It is your responsibility to set boundaries against negative thinking and negative attitudes, focus on the find-a-way mentality, and build a culture of optimism and proactivity.[16] Encourage team members who disagreed with the decision to commit now to making it a success. Remind them that their points of view were put on the table and considered. Now, everyone needs to trust in the collective wisdom of the team and let go of their own individual ideas or reservations.

Actions

Thinking must be translated into actions. Those actions, in turn, need to be aligned with the direction set. Most leaders are doers. You got to the position you're in because you could make things happen—you're not lazy! Although grass is not likely growing under your feet, weeds very well may be.

I asked members of a team I was coaching in the Middle East this question: "What defines a successful day?" They thought for a moment and then shared the company line of engaging in the accomplishment of their mission statement. I challenged them to reconsider their answer, because I had observed otherwise over a few months. In my observation of their actions, their *actual* definition of a successful day was how busy they had been—how many phone messages, emails, texts, and tweets they had been able to knock off their to-do list. From what I saw, they felt successful if they hit the ground running each morning and maintained a rapid pace throughout the day. They conceded that I was probably right.

Busy with the Right Things

My wife and I toured the Ford Motor Company in Detroit, Michigan, years ago. I have always been fascinated with how things are made. The tour began with the assembly line, which was a quarter of a mile long. As we began our journey, two axles were placed on the belt. We walked alongside those axles as they continued down the line. As we glanced ahead, we saw what seemed to be an endless flurry of activity.

---

16 Cloud, *Boundaries for Leaders*, 122.

People and machines were adding parts every step of the way. There was motion everywhere. What at first seemed almost chaotic was actually a well-orchestrated symphony. At one point, the chassis was mounted. Seats were included. The motor was installed. Wheels and tires were applied. To our amazement, at the end of all that enterprise, someone actually got into a complete car and drove it off. That quarter-of-a-mile-long assembly line was not merely a beehive of activity. All the hustle produced what it was designed to produce—a working car that was ready for the consumer.

Dawson Trotman, the founder of the organization for which I work, is known for saying, "Activity is no substitute for production." As the Ford factory example illustrates, you can have both—productive activity. But you can also have activity that's getting you nowhere. The real question is not how busy people are, but how busy they are doing the right things. Actions are important, and not just any actions will do. Henry Cloud put it this way: "Actions are the right things done in the right way at the right time that build momentum and get results."[17] Notice the intentionality in this statement through the use of the word "right." Alignment of actions doesn't refer to mere activity. The actions need to be the *right* ones—at the *right* time, in the *right* way—that will drive success. (By the way, this doesn't mean there is only one possible *right* action at any given time; there could be a range of equally valid options, but they still need to be ones that get you where you're trying to go.) Cloud goes on to urge, "In the list of actions that your people can control, have them find the ones that *actually affect outcomes*."[18] Again, this is not to say there is only one way or that the right way is "my way." The definition of "right actions" is that they achieve the results desired.

I was helping a leader in Canada, John, who had hired a recruiter (Bob was his name) for his organization. After a year on the job, Bob had recruited just one new hire. I asked John if this met his definition of success. He said it didn't and was trying to figure out how to help Bob do a better job. I asked John how he was thinking he might help Bob. He said he was going to ask him to spend more time in the office rather than working from his home.

---

17 Cloud, *Boundaries for Leaders*, 147–148.

18 Cloud, *Boundaries for Leaders*, 148. Italics are in the original.

"John, let's think about that a moment," I responded. "Let's say Bob does exactly what you ask of him, but he spends most of the time in the office playing video games on his smartphone. He is doing what you wanted, but it's still not helping to build momentum and get results!"

John saw my point. I continued, "What would be the right things done in the right way at the right time to get what you need from Bob?" Together, we then broke down the questions he should ask to ensure Bob could succeed.

- **Right results**: What are you after? (Answer: Recruit new staff to join the team.)
- **Right actions**: What does Bob need to be doing to be successful at achieving this result? What are the two or three things he *must* be doing?
- **Right way**: Of these two or three key things Bob needs to be doing, what is the best way to do each one? For example, if making recruiting presentations is one of the right things he should be doing, what is the best way to make a presentation? Should it be one-on-one? To a small group or a large group? Is it best to make a presentation with printed materials or with PowerPoint? What should the materials and presentations include?
- **Right time**: Of the right things done the right way, what is the best sequencing of those actions? What should be done first? Which action should follow? Since he would be recruiting on college campuses, what are the best times of the school year to be on campus?

Resources

The third area of alignment is resources: providing the right tools and materials needed for success. A simple example illustrates the importance of the need to have resources aligned. Let's say you're in an enterprising mood and decide to make your favorite recipe for angel food cake. You start mixing together the necessary ingredients. However, you are short one resource—egg whites. It's just one item (well, technically a dozen—but one carton!). You have everything else you need. However, no matter how much of the other ingredients you have on hand, without eggs you'll never be able to make that angel food cake.

Resources are a lot like the egg whites in an angel food cake. When I was a regional director for an international corporation, my supervisor and mentor, Paul Stanley, knew the important role resources could play in new initiatives. He had set aside a portion of his budget for what he called his "initiatives fund." No one knew he had this fund, and he used it both sparingly and strategically. He has always been great at asking questions. He would often ask questions concerning new approaches to our work, always trying to discover what people were thinking about and working toward. He would then ask his familiar question: "What's holding you back from pulling that off?" The reply was often resources (a lack thereof, that is). Paul would continue with, "If you had the funds, how would you use them to complete this idea?" With a satisfactory answer, he would send a check. He didn't fund the entire project. That was the responsibility of the person creating it. However, his timely generosity would knock down that final obstacle that was preventing the project from becoming a reality.

The lack of attention to resources is a common mistake. Asking these questions can be helpful:

1. What resources are required for success?
2. What are their costs?
3. How can they be acquired?
4. What is the deadline for securing them?
5. Who will take responsibility for obtaining them?

People

The fourth area of alignment is people—specifically, getting the right people in the right responsibilities. Some may argue that people are one kind of resource (human resources). While this is true, people are fundamentally different than material resources, and it's helpful to delineate these two areas.

Getting people in the right spots on your team is about much more than putting their names on an organizational chart. The operative word, again, is "right." Who are the *right* people who can actually drive actions, add value through their strengths and experience, and execute your plans well?

To help find the right person for a particular role or task, my friend Jess MacCallum has developed a simple but effective tool called the Leader Selection Chart, which you'll find in part III. The grid helps you consider both the organization's needs and the individual's qualifications.

———————

Setting the right direction is tough. Bringing everyone and everything into alignment with that direction is even tougher. Naturally, tendencies are to assume too much, to drift, and to scatter as a team. Alignment requires intentionality and hard work. It is not about conformity but togetherness in thinking, actions, resources, and people.

Chapter 6 Key Takeaways:

- Alignment, the second Operational Aspect of Lead, is about bringing together. It does not necessarily mean everyone will agree with every decision, but that all views are heard and considered.
- As a leader, your challenge is to align the thinking, actions, resources, and people on your team.
- A big part of alignment is ensuring that your people are busy with the right activities at the right time and in the right way.
- The Leader Selection Chart is a tool to help you with aligning the people you lead.

Chapter 7
Lead Operational Aspect #3: Motivate

Max is an executive in his early thirties working for a multimillion-dollar company in Asia. We looked at who he was leading.

"So how motivated is John [one of his direct reports]?"

"Not very," Max said.

"Where would you put him on a scale of one to ten for motivation?"

"Oh, around five or six."

"What effect is his medium-level motivation having on his performance in his role?"

"He does what is required of him," Max explained. "He meets the deadlines for his work. But I don't really see him and his personality in what he produces. It seems we get the minimum. I just know there is more of himself, of his creativity, that he could put into what he does."

We asked Max, "What do you think the solution is?"

"I don't want more hours," he quickly said. "It's not a matter of quantity but of quality. I'm confident he has the capacity, because I've seen it before from him, but he's just not bringing it to his work anymore. It's like his thought and creativity have gone missing."

Max knew what wouldn't work, but he was still searching for a solution, so we continued with this question: "What do you think motivates John?"

"You know, I don't really know," Max said, seemingly surprised that he hadn't asked himself that question before.

"How could you find out?" we asked.

One of the most important tasks of a leader is to influence and motivate those he or she leads to not only do what needs to be done, but also to *tap into their energy* to do it. Motivation is the "wind in the sails." You can manipulate people with bribes and threats, but ideally, the best kind of motivation is the kind that comes from within. You want those you lead to be driven by a deeper source of energy.

People are more than animals. We don't just avoid pain and pursue pleasure, carrying out our lives based on pure reflex. The deeper motivation or instinct to *create*—whether it's ideas, art, products, good in another's life, or something else—is uniquely human. When genuinely motivated, a person is willing and able to sacrifice much. But you have to find a way to tap into that enormous potential if it lies (or has suddenly gone) dormant.

Four Motivating Factors

What are some of these deeper desires that will help you motivate your people?

- **Life**—Everyone wants to really "live" life.
- **Relationships**—No one wants to be all alone. We all long for true intimacy.
- **Growth**—People long to reach their true potential.
- **Purpose**—We all want who we are and what we do to make a difference in the larger scheme of life and history.

The leader's challenge is to help make the connection between people's deepest and best motivations and the tasks to be done. As someone has said so well, "Vision is tying their story to a larger story."[19] It is amazing what highly motivated people can accomplish. You don't have to drive them—just guide them. They are a force to be reckoned with.

Mother Teresa was a classic example of what can happen when a person realizes her motivation. She began her work teaching school at the Loreto Convent School in Entally in eastern Calcutta, India, in 1937. She served there for nearly twenty years and was appointed headmistress in 1944.

---

19 An anonymous quote.

LEAD DEVELOP CARE

Although Teresa enjoyed teaching at the school, she was increasingly disturbed by the poverty and suffering surrounding her in Calcutta. People were literally dying outside the windows of her classroom. Increasingly motivated to help, she reached a turning point in her life when she shared that she simply could not "*not* go out there to them." Her bishop agreed and released her to her motivation, which eventually led to the founding of the Missionaries of Charity, aimed at caring for those who had become a burden to society and were shunned by everyone. What started with her and a handful of sisters today has involved thousands. This diminutive giant even received the Nobel Peace Prize for her sacrificial care. Her life's work and legacy are an inspiring illustration of unleashed motivation.

Giving Motivation More Attention

Of the four Operational Aspects of Lead, Motivate may get the least attention. Perhaps we take it for granted, especially in a workplace setting. "We tell them what to do and give them a salary. Shouldn't that be enough?" But maybe you've noticed, a paycheck will only go so far in terms of motivation; it doesn't tap into that inner spring of desire and creativity, so ultimately, a person—to truly contribute to the best of their ability—needs a greater and higher drive from within.

If you're not sure what motivates those you lead, start by asking yourself what motivates *you*? Have you even given that question much thought? What gets you up in the morning? What *keeps* you going, especially on those hard days when nothing's going as planned?

Make no mistake, your ability to motivate your people is one of your most important contributions as a leader. In his book *Start With Why*, Simon Sinek pushes motivation to the top of the list as a priority for leaders:

> Just about every person or organization needs to motivate others to act for some reason or another. Some want to motivate a purchase decision. Others are looking for support or a vote. Still others are keen to motivate the people around them to work harder or smarter or just follow the rules. The ability to motivate people is not, in itself, difficult. It is usually tied to some external factor. Tempting incentives or the threat of punishment will

often elicit the behavior we desire … It's worth repeating: people don't buy WHAT you do, they buy WHY you do it.[20]

The critical nature of motivation can be seen very clearly when you lead a family with teenagers (as I have!). How do you motivate a fourteen-year-old to clean up his room? How do you motivate a sixteen-year-old to do her homework instead of chatting on social media? Whoever figures out the answers to those kinds of questions will make a lot of money! In all seriousness, though, we too often rely on bribes or threats, instead of doing the harder work of trying to tap into the motivations of the heart. And great leaders are willing to put in the effort.

Unleashing Motivation

Before shifting into a leader development career, I taught eighth-grade English. I loved teaching; however, I had a ton of students who were not very motivated. They reminded me a lot of when I was their same age.

One of my students was named Mike. As we started the school year, it was apparent that Mike was a bit older than the other eighth graders. I asked other teachers about him. It turned out that he was three years older than the other students because of his poor academic progress. He didn't seem to have any mental or learning disabilities, but he was still behind everyone.

I wanted to help Mike along with other students who were struggling with my class. I began to use my free period to tutor students who were available to come in during that time. Each day, I'd have twenty to twenty-five students sitting at their desks or standing at the blackboards (yes, those were the days of chalk!) diagramming sentences to learn the basics of syntax. I didn't realize it at the time, but this created a relatively safe environment for these students. Representing a cross-section of the social fabric of the school, the students who came during this drop-in period all had one thing in common: they didn't know how to write very well.

We worked hard but also had fun. We took concepts one step at a time. Success was defined not by who could complete the diagram the quick-

---

20 Simon Sinek, *Start with Why: How Great Leaders Inspire Everyone to Take Action* (New York: Portfolio/Penguin, 2009), 5–6, 4. See also http://startwithwhy.com.

est but by who was making progress. Students would go from not even being able to identify the subject and verb in a sentence to being able to label both correctly. We played games to learn. I let those who were getting it a bit faster help their friends who had not quite caught up with them. You could see the satisfaction on their faces as they slowly realized that they had something to give to others.

Each of these periods, I'd also share a thought for the day. One time, I shared that as human beings, they were God's highest creation. That idea carried two significant implications for these students. First, they had inherent worth and dignity and should always be treated as such. Second, they were unique, and each had a contribution to make that only he or she could make.

In this safe environment, I began to see students' motivation for writing (and even in seeing that they could help each other) change. Mike began to break out of the cocoon he had created around himself at his desk. He would get up and stand at the blackboard in front of everyone, and he even began helping friends with their sentence diagrams. As the year progressed, he went from being a D or F student to making the straight-A honor roll. His other teachers were dumbfounded but wonderfully pleased.

I asked Mike one day about his story through his school years. He shared with me that when he was in second grade, he had done something in class that prompted his teacher's ire. Maybe she was just having a bad day (I had my moments in the classroom as well!), but the way she handled Mike's behavior had a long-lasting, negative impact: she had him stand in front of his class and then, in so many words, told the class how stupid and dumb he was. Mike failed the next three grades. His subsequent teachers, as well-meaning and hard-working as they were, started each school year with knowledge of Mike's background. This (perhaps unintentionally for some) affected how they treated him. When I came on board for my first year of teaching, I had not heard about Mike's past, so it couldn't color how I treated him. By creating a safe place for him to grow and succeed, I'd helped him see the rewards of hard work and the potential to contribute positively to others. His motivation to excel was unleashed.

Steps Toward Motivation

We suggest four practical steps forward from here:

1. Take some time to think about what motivates *and* demotivates you.
2. Think about each of the people you lead. How motivated are they? What motivates them? What demotivates them?
3. Think of ways to get better answers to these questions.
4. Evaluate your stated mission and vision. How compelling is that? How can you "tie your people's story to a larger story"?

As the leader, you're uniquely placed to motivate your people. They take their cue from you. And for starters, it is extremely motivating for people to be well led!

Extrinsic and Intrinsic Motivators

Edward Deci, in his book, *Why We Do What We Do: The Dynamics of Personal Autonomy*, asks a key question, "How can I create the conditions within which people will motivate themselves?"[21] To get at the answer, we need to understand how people are generally motivated. He points out that we as humans are motivated both extrinsically and intrinsically. Modern motivational literature based on Deci's research and popularized by motivational speakers such as Simon Sinek explains these two basic motivational platforms using eight key motivations that they see manifested in today's work world. Others could be listed, of course, but these provide a good and comprehensive start.

Extrinsic motivations:

- Rewards—What do I/we gain if I/we win?
- Consequences—What do I/we lose if I/we fail?
- Security—Are my responses to people safe, consistent, and for their development?
- Appreciation—Am I recognized for my contribution?

---

21 Penguin Random House, "About Why We Do What We Do," www.penguinrandomhouse.com/books/335221/.

Intrinsic motivations:

- Empowerment—Will you let me do it?
- Development—Will this enable me to get better at something?
- Purpose—Is this tied to a bigger story?
- Competition—Can I test my abilities against peers?

The Motivate Tool in part III is organized by these eight motivations, and I highly recommend you use that tool to help you take steps toward motivating those you lead.

In summary, motivation is for humans—real people who live in a real world—not machines. We are complex creatures with inherent abilities to use and contributions to make. We also have insecurities and fears that may limit us. The Trusted Leader recognizes this and works hard at unleashing his or her own motivations as well as those of others.

Chapter 7 Key Takeaways:

- Motivate is the third Operational Aspect of Lead and is perhaps the one to which leaders pay the least attention.
- Leaders are in a unique position to motivate people, and motivation can be one of their most important contributions.
- Motivation is about far more than money and other tangibles. There are both extrinsic and intrinsic motivations; you should consider these as a team and individually to ensure your activities are energizing and not draining.

Chapter 8
Lead Operational Aspect #4: Manage

It had been just over three years since John had joined his company as its database manager. The staff was relatively small, so it surprised John that he almost never saw his supervisor, Chuck, who was also the founder and president. John's job description was clear enough, and the overall vision of the organization was very motivating to him, but over time he began to be bothered that he had virtually no contact with his boss except when there was something Chuck didn't like. He knew Chuck had a general idea about what he was doing, but he never took the time to discuss it with John or interact with him on how he could do it better.

Early in his tenure on the job, John saw Chuck walk into the office one day, and he made a point to go into the coffee/break room at the same time as him. As soon as John walked in and was on the verge of making a friendly greeting, Chuck glanced John's direction, mumbled "hello," and hurried out. John saw him go into the vice president's office for a bit, then leave the office. These types of incidents recurred, and in those three years, he'd talked to Chuck one-on-one a total of maybe fifteen minutes. He'd understand if this were a large corporation, but there were fewer than twenty staff members—and it's not as though the office setup should've prevented a more collegial relationship.

Over time, John felt abandoned and devalued. When he hit his four-year mark with the organization, he decided to leave and take a job elsewhere.

You may be thinking, "I thought this was a book on leadership. Why a chapter on management?" That's a fair question. After all, leadership and management are two different concepts with two different functions. Leading is more future-oriented and focused on the big ideas while managing is more now-oriented with a focus on the details. But the two concepts are best viewed as two wings of the same airplane. They need to be treated and maintained separately while held in a dynamic tension, each dependent on the other. Another way to put it is that, as a leader, you need to both lead people and manage their work.

I love casting vision and inspiring, setting direction and motivating. But to be honest, I'm not great with details and often don't think things all the way through from start to finish. What are the costs? What are the threats we need to anticipate? What if my starting assumptions are wrong?

As I am future-oriented, I can get distracted from the present and sometimes drop the ball in the faithful execution of key tasks from day to day. Fortunately, my wife is very down to earth and attuned to the details. So, if we work together, we bring the full complement of the four operational aspects of Lead.

With Set Direction, you launch the enterprise. It's a key responsibility of leadership. However, many leaders feel that, once they've done that, everything will fall into place. In fact, just the opposite can (and too often does) happen—everything falls apart. As the saying goes, the devil is in the details. Just because you start well does not guarantee you will finish well. Someone needs to "mind the store" and stay on top of all the parts and pieces. Stuff happens. Problems arise. Unexpected opportunities open up. People quit. Something breaks. And so on. Sometimes these developments necessitate a course adjustment, setting a *new* direction. This, in turn, will require a new alignment and perhaps a renewal of motivation. In all of this, your strategic presence as the leader is a vital part of managing the work.

Being Present

What does it mean to "be present" as a leader? People generally don't want you to hover or micromanage. But on the other hand, resentment can occur (as it did with John in the opening story) if the people you are leading feel like you have abandoned them. Effective management involves bringing structure and accountability, so your presence is important.

I was working with one leader, Andre, who led a team dispersed across a multinational geographical region. Andre's means of managing his country leaders was via reports. Monthly and quarterly reports were dutifully submitted by those on his team. Now, reports have their place. However, leaders who depend heavily on reports frequently do so because they really don't know what's going on out in the field. The reports give them a feeling that they *do* know what's going on, though this is often an illusion if the reports are all those leaders have to go on.

Being hired to help Andre and his team grow as effective leaders, I began with our usual approach of presenting our leadership model to his team of country leaders in a symposium. I followed up by scheduling an on-site visit with each one of the leaders, so I could get to know them better, the challenges and opportunities they faced, and meet the other people with whom they led. I took several days for each visit, primarily because this region was overseas for me and I knew I had to gather all the intelligence I could on these visits. (For a leader whose team is on-site, or at least very close together in geography, being present will look different.)

After one of these visits with a country leader named Frederic, I was briefing Andre on what I'd learned. After I shared some observations, I recommended ways to help Frederic develop as a leader, including a key area of needed personal growth. Andre looked surprised and asked me, "How in the world did you discover that as an area of needed improvement?" I explained that, besides my five days with his entire team, I had had many hours of travel time with Frederic. The area of need was obvious from all of this interaction I'd had with him.

I then asked Andre, "How long has Frederic been on your team?"

"Seven years," he replied.

"In those seven years, how many times have you traveled with Frederic or been with him and his teammates?" I asked.

"None," Andre admitted, frowning.

I reinforced for Andre right then that one cannot lead and manage people well from behind a computer screen. Even with the advantages of video chatting, actual presence is still needed.

Actual presence, in moderation, communicates interest and care. It provides insights and observations that cannot otherwise be gathered. It is critically important.

Being present does involve that dreaded task of *meeting*. You've probably heard of "death by meeting" (Patrick Lencioni wrote a great book by the same title). Determining your meetings' frequency, length, and purpose—and being intentional and communicative about these aspects of your meetings—will help reduce the dread. And by all means, don't meet just to meet. Many fine books have covered this topic, so I won't dwell on it; in addition to the Lencioni one, I recommend *Leading from the Sandbox* (T. J. Addington) and *The Four Disciplines of Execution* (Chris McChesney, Sean Covey, and Jim Huling).

Dealing with the Unexpected

Managing also entails dealing with unexpected events and problems that arise. Is it necessary to change direction? What are we going to do about this new obstacle we're facing? These are the kinds of questions you as the leader need to ask and answer.

As dramatized in the movie by the same name, Apollo 13 was the seventh manned mission in the Apollo space program and the third intended to land on the moon. It was launched on April 11, 1970, from the Kennedy Space Center in Florida, but two days later an oxygen tank exploded, crippling the service module. The original direction set was to land on the moon, but with this unexpected accident, the goal quickly shifted to just trying to get the men home safely. The situation had to be managed. Given the new realities, what were the crew members going to do? How were they going to do it? And despite great hardship caused by limited power, loss of cabin heat, shortage of potable water, and the critical need to make makeshift repairs to the carbon-dioxide-removal system, the crew returned safely to Earth six days after launch. What a spectacular example of the importance of managing an unexpected turn of events!

Another classic illustration of the importance of dealing with the unexpected is seen in the movie *Gettysburg*. Colonel Joshua Lawrence Chamberlain and his regiment from Maine find themselves holding the end of the line on Little Round Top. Having repelled several Confederate attacks, he and his men are exhausted, out of ammunition, and about to face another charge by the Confederate forces. As he pulls his leaders together, they are seen standing around him, their facial expressions all asking the same question of him: "What are we going to do?" Colonel Chamberlain's men can't file a report at the moment. They can't submit a written proposal. They are in need, plain and simple, as they face an unexpected situation. And fortunately for them, their leader was present and able to give the directive and plan that enabled them to be successful in the defense of their position.

Evaluating Honestly

Managing also involves taking an honest look at whether or not you and your team are really getting the job done. In many work settings a structured approach to regular evaluation includes some kind of year-end plan and progress review along with regular team meetings that keep people in touch with the big picture. People tend to drift and need to be brought back into alignment with the overall stated purpose. It is important to get the team's input, because other people will see things you don't see due to their varied gifts, abilities, and experiences.

I find these questions helpful in evaluating people:

- What are your responsibilities?
- What does it look like to do those responsibilities well?
- How competent and confident do you feel in doing them?
- What would increase your competence and confidence?
- What is your plan to get that development?
- How can I help?

Stewarding the Future *and* Present

Staying on top of day-to-day operations is very important for you as the leader. You are responsible for the present state of your office, organization, family, or whatever you lead. But you're not *only* manager of the here and now; you're also a steward of the future. So, it's important to ask questions such as:

- Where are you, as an organization, headed in the next five to ten years?
- How are you and the team looking ahead to anticipate change, plan for growth, and mitigate potential threats?

Four ways to ensure you're managing both the present and the future well include planning, organizing, guiding, and assessing.

Planning

An ancient proverb says that the plans of the diligent lead surely to abundance, but everyone who is hasty comes only to poverty (Proverbs 21:5). Planning, at its core, is thinking through and writing down ahead of time where you want to find yourself later. It is not a guarantee of accomplishment. Your product (the plan) is not as important as the process. As General Dwight D. Eisenhower said, "Plans are useless, but planning is indispensable."[22] Another adage, attributed to a host of military leaders, states that "no plan survives contact with the enemy."

The process of planning enables you to not be caught completely by surprise by the current realities. Having thought-through directions and contingencies helps the possibilities of success.

There is a plethora of planning tools, techniques, and exercises available. My recommendation is to find the one that works for you. Whether it's using the latest technological gadget or simply writing plans on a napkin at the coffee shop, it's important to use what works for you. I find that the real key to planning is not the tool but the time: time away from distractions; time to reflect; time to review; time to get above the fray and see your situation from the 30,000-foot view. My suggestion to leaders is to carve out a block of time each week for planning. Don't use the usual excuse of "not being able to find the time for this"; for something so important, you have to find the time!

Organizing

My wife and I participated in a workday project at our granddaughter's school. The scope of the projects we were to work on was wide and varied, from picking up trash in the parking lot, to planting flowers in a butterfly area, to repairing the playground equipment for the kindergarten kids. When we had over fifty volunteers show up, I was wondering how the ones leading the project were going to get us organized. I needn't have worried. The leader broke us into teams, told us what our tasks were, directed us to the pickup truck loaded with the necessary tools, and then led us to our various sites for the work.

---

22 From a speech to the National Defense Executive Reserve Conference in Washington, DC (November 14, 1957), in D. Eisenhower, *Public Papers of the Presidents of the United States*, National Archives and Records Service, Government Printing Office, 1957, 818.

I was thinking it would take at least an hour just to get started. Instead, it took a matter of minutes. Jim Collins, in his bestselling book *Good to Great*, wrote, "It is better to first get the right people on the bus, the wrong people off the bus, and the right people in the right seats, and then figure out where to drive."[23]

This doesn't just happen. Substantial planning and organizing must take place first. Much of that process takes place behind the scenes without those on the outside ever realizing it's happened! We can read online about two country leaders meeting together and having a successful summit over a two-day period. The news articles make it sound so simple—like those two important people simply met up and chatted. The reality is that that type of meeting doesn't only take a couple of days. Weeks and months of planning and organizing took place beforehand.

The effort it takes to organize well can be a significant challenge for many leaders, especially the visionary ones. Often, leaders come up short in trying to translate what is in their heads to tangible steps others can follow.

Guiding

People need to know guidelines for what's expected of them. They don't need the leader to do the work for them (that should not happen!). Guiding is not micromanaging. Laying down guidelines involves providing just enough assistance to enable people to reach the desired destination. Guiding also involves setting boundaries. On what do you want those you lead to focus, and on what do you *not* want them to focus? Direct reports tend to have about a half-dozen specific guidance questions for their supervisors. A list of these questions (provided in the form of statements) is part of Manage Tool #1 in part III.

Assessing

Finally, people need to know how they're doing. In fact, they *want* to know ... sort of. Actually, for most of us, we have a love/hate relationship with feedback. We want to know if we are on track (is what we're doing what the leader wanted?). At the same time, evaluation touches on

---

23 Jim Collins, *Good to Great: Why Some Companies Make the Leap … and Others Don't* (New York: HarperBusiness, 2011), 41.

the insecurities we all have. We all want to do well and succeed and be well regarded. Yet, we also know there is always room for improvement.

I have found that there are two types of evaluation that are really needed and helpful. One assessment is from leaders: how they sense things are going. That perspective is very important as their perspective shapes all they do. Any building upon or suggesting of adjustments will be based on how the leader sees things.

The second assessment is from those being led—how *they* sense things are going. Now, this may sound like the leader's view is not to be trusted. As a coach of leaders, I do trust that the leaders are telling me their perspective; generally, I'm confident that they are not trying to deceive me. Yet, their view is still just that—their point of view. And as the baseball umpire says, "I call them as I see them." But how the leader sees reality may not be the full story.

I was brought into a large multinational organization to help with leader development. My work began with a three-day, off-site meeting with the company's ten-member executive team. We talked about how they felt the work was going, how they were doing as leaders, and how their staff viewed them as leaders. Overall, it was a positive report. The executive team members communicated their care for their respective teams. They took their leadership roles seriously. They all felt that those they led appreciated their work.

After the executive team meeting, several hundred of the rest of the staff gathered for the organization's annual conference. Attending the event, I shifted my attention from the executive team to the field staff. I had a set of questions that I asked twenty-three staff members with whom I was able to meet one-on-one for coffee over a couple of days (I knew none of these staff members before the conference). It was amazing, though (based on my experience) unsurprising, how different their viewpoints were from those of their leaders. Rather than appreciating their leaders, for example, some of the staff felt their jobs were to protect their people from the company leadership. Talk about a contrast of perspectives!

What was the problem? Perspective. As stated earlier, we have to honestly evaluate reality, which requires a more comprehensive approach from all sides. Built into our makeup from birth is the desire to do well and to please those who hold a place of importance in our lives. We mean well. We try hard. We want to succeed and make a contribution. Yet, like a bobsled hurling down its course, we keep bumping the sides slowing us down. And at times, when the walls that we've constructed to keep us on course are disregarded, we can fly off the track entirely. Good assessment is like those bumps along the sides of our lives: a reminder that we're drifting too far one way or another, that we may be making good speed but off-track (whether by a little or a lot).

Chapter 8 Key Takeaways:

- Leadership and management are often seen as rivals; leaders tend to look with disdain at the "bean counters" while managers roll their eyes at the latest "vision from on high." Instead, it's best to see these areas as complementary, necessary collaborators.
- Some leaders tend to set direction, then "delegate and abdicate." A leader has the responsibility to be present and oversee adjustments in course needed along the way (e.g., when unexpected circumstances arise).
- You need to manage the present and steward the future; the latter entails planning, organizing, guiding, and assessing.

The LDC model integrates interrelated actions, which should be combined and carried out with intentionality, undergirded by a shepherd's heart for the people you lead.

Lead: Operational Aspect Summary

Set Direction, Align, Motivate, and **Manage** constitute the foundational actions for Leading well. All four of these aspects of Lead are important individually; interrelated, their integration is even more vital. Alignment naturally flows out of a clear, agreed-upon direction and ensures that a diversity of people and opinions can come togeth-

er, get "on the same page," and work toward a common goal. Leaders who harness the power of Motivation unleash energy and commitment that contribute to greater success in every other area. Management involves stewardship of both the present and the future so that resources (whether finances, materials, or precious energy and time) are not wasted or underutilized.

In Action

Mark's coach, Bob, felt he had clearly articulated their team's target. The team was busy with a flurry of activity. Mark and other team members' efforts were even fueled with high levels of motivation. Still, the team was not making much progress toward the goal. Engaging in conversation with each team member, Bob was sure he would uncover alignment issues. Instead, he was surprised to find that the real issue was with direction. Apparently, their target had not been as clearly understood as he thought. Every team member had a slightly different understanding of their end goal, and of what it would look like when they accomplished it. Only one or two degrees off-center meant the team was in danger of missing the target completely.

Chapter 9
Develop Operational Aspect #1: Discover

The response of the department head, Marie, was all too familiar. I had asked her a simple question: "As you think of your team, could you brief me on the specific area of development you're working on with each person?"

"Oh, they're actually doing well," she replied. "I don't have any significant problems with any of my team members at the moment. It's been quite enjoyable to be in such an easy place with them."

I then asked Marie how she viewed the responsibility of developing her team. "Is it primarily about looking out for problems and responding to whatever pops up?" I asked her. "Is it more reactive than proactive? Is it something that just happens? Or should there be a thought-through schematic for each person's development?"

Marie replied that she hadn't really given this responsibility much thought, but she was confident that every experience has the potential to be developmental. She believed that the more experiences she could give her team members, the more they would grow and develop. They all had several years on the team; she was sure all those years of experience were paying off somehow.

I pointed to one person's name on the list of her team—Matt. "What has been Matt's primary focus this past year?" I asked. She shared that he had the main responsibility of marketing one of the company's new products. He had been in the role for a year and was doing well.

"That's encouraging to hear. I'm glad it's been a good experience for him," I replied. "Now, could you qualify specifically why it's been a 'good experience' for him? How would you finish the sentence, 'Through this experience, I have seen Matt develop in …'?"

Predictably, Marie faltered in her response. She was confident Matt had grown. To be sure, he had faced challenges along the way—some bumps in the road; but overall, he had enjoyed some successes. She was sure Matt had learned something through the process.

I asked her again if she could highlight one or two of those development areas for me.

"Well, I'll need to give that some more thought," she replied, with a tinge of embarrassment that she could not move beyond vague statements.

Moving Past the Development Assumption

After initial orientation training takes place, personal and professional development tends to be more accidental than intentional, more episodic than continual. Over decades of experience, I've observed a pervasive "development assumption." It's often articulated something like this: "Surely they are picking up some important things from their experiences." (This was exactly the assumption of Marie in the story that introduced this chapter.)

In other words, many leaders take a reactive rather than proactive approach to developing their people. It might even be described as a lazy approach.

To get beyond this development assumption, it's critical to start with a clear view of the target rather than hoping some new perspective or skill gets magically picked up. We have to intentionally discover or identify what we're aiming to Develop.

Starting the Development Discovery Process

A lot of professional development training is very specific. To train someone how to fly an airplane, for instance, there is a determined schematic for the topics, procedures, sequences, and skills required. However, not all role/job training is as specific or straightforward.

How do you train someone to improve in "people skills," decision-making, or teamwork? Certain "soft skills" like these require a measure of emotional intelligence that can be difficult to develop in others.

(Emotional intelligence is the ability to understand and manage your emotions and those of the people around you. Its four prongs include self-awareness, self-management, social awareness, and relationship management.)

Besides these challenges, there's need for a game plan for *your specific* team and its individuals. This need, of course, must be balanced in light of competing priorities and limited time. (Realistically, creating detailed, customized development plans for every direct report can be time-consuming and is not always feasible for leaders who supervise large numbers of people.)

Determining exactly *what* to develop a particular person in can feel daunting—the sheer number of possibilities is endless. Yet, it's vital that you develop the people you lead in relevant ways—in areas in which they actually need to be developed to do their jobs well.

As leaders, we can't rely on the omnibus "annual development seminar" that lets us check off a box for the year. We have to stop reaching blindly into our grab-bag of tips and tricks, tools and techniques, hoping the one we pick that day will help.

Besides being specific and relevant, development needs to be as comprehensive as possible. In short, any development plan needs to be both doable and effective. And, as mentioned above, it needs to address both soft skills and hard skills.

Following are several tips to Discover (identify) areas of needed development, beginning with consideration of three development essentials followed by recommendations for questions to ask to apply them.

The Development Essentials: Thinking, Behavior, Skills

Before you embark on Development Discovery, it's important to think in terms of major categories of development. This helps clear the clutter of details and focus on what matters most.

I was traveling on a bus in southern Mexico some years ago with a group of colleagues. As we snaked our way through the thick jungle terrain enveloping us, we found our eyes darted from side to side as we scanned the plethora of trees, plants, flowers, creeks, valleys, and varieties of birds. We were almost overwhelmed with the detail. As we continued to climb in elevation, we hit a fog bank that obliterated our sight. A few minutes later, as the bus continued its upward journey, we emerged from the fog. It was an amazing sight as we looked around. Instead of the dense jungle with its staggering visage, all we could see were a handful of mountain peaks, like islands popping up out of water. The fog bank below us eliminated our view of everything under it.

Similarly, there are only a handful of development "mountaintops." I look for these peaks first when I consider developing others. They help me get my bearings—understand the overall landscape—even if a lot of the details are still submerged in fog.

I call these mountaintops the development essentials, and they include thinking, behavior, and skills. In fact, every area of development can find a home under one of these three areas or a combination of them. Let's look at each one in more detail.

Thinking

Thinking deals with a person's understanding and presuppositions; it's the grid through which someone sees and understands everything in their lives. Every action (and inaction) stems from thoughts. Every belief and value finds its genesis in our thinking. How we carry ourselves and how we respond to challenges (confidently tackling versus fearfully fleeing) result from our thinking—whether consciously or subconsciously. The same is true for how we treat others and how we handle our responsibilities.

Thinking is so important to development because it reveals the barriers to development. It shows what's holding us back.

One fall day, one of my young grandsons was riding his bicycle in our driveway. He had the training wheels on, giving him extra confidence. The smile on his face revealed how much he was enjoying himself. Nearby, I was raking leaves. I thought he might enjoy something more than just riding his bike on the pavement. I decided to rake a huge pile of leaves onto the driveway. I then asked him if he would like to ride his bike through the pile. I was a bit surprised when he shook his head "no." I asked, "Why not?" Hesitantly, he replied, "It's too big, Papa." I responded, "If I hold on to you and your bike and go with you through the pile of leaves, would you want to try it?" He lit up: "You'll go with me?" "Yes," I assured him, "I'll go with you." He said, "OK, I'll try it."

I grabbed the seat of the bike and the handlebars and began pushing him. "Here we go!" I said. And away we went toward the large pile. Within one second of blasting through the leaves, he was shouting, "Let's do it again, Papa! Let's do it again!"

What had changed? What caused my grandson to go from a fearful "No, it's too big" to a courageous "Let's do it again"? It wasn't a newfound skill that he gained; he could ride the bike already. It wasn't his behavior that changed either (at least not yet). What changed was his thinking: he went from thinking the pile of leaves was too big to thinking it was do-able (and even fun) to ride through it. His fearful thinking had initially hindered his development as a bike rider. But once he rode through the pile with me holding on, he instantly thought differently. Focusing on reshaping his thinking enabled his development as a bike rider.

Behavior

Behavior includes a person's actions and reactions, their attitudes and conduct.

Like thinking, behavior can be a tough development area to deal with. In today's culture especially, we generally don't like pointing out people's wrongdoings, either privately or publicly. We're scared of how they will react. We're afraid to be labeled "judgmental." We may hold back from saying anything about a person's behavior, thinking, "That's just the way he/she is." We may wish a person wouldn't be so difficult to be around, but if the company really needs that individual, we excuse or grudgingly overlook misbehavior. This type of bottom-line approach can be detrimental in the long run. In case after case, we've seen a single team member's troublesome behavior become the factor that brings down an entire team and its leader.

It's to a leader's peril to neglect behavior—not only team members' behavior but his or her own. In fact, a leader's poor behavior is what *usually* pulls him or her down—it's the Achilles' heel that causes the leader to fall. Not dealing with behavior issues will damage a leader and the many others on whom they currently have or will have an impact.

A scene in the movie *Master and Commander* (2003) illustrates this point well. During a massive storm, one of the sailors is up on the mast trying to secure the sail. However, the mast and sail give way to violent winds and fall into the sea, and the sailor falls along with them. All the rigging is still connected to the ship. The ropes are his only way of being saved. Everyone is yelling for him to get back to the ship. However, all the rigging is acting as a sea anchor. The ship, with everyone on it, is beginning to roll over and capsize.

Amidst a desire to save the one sailor, the captain and officers are faced with a dreadful dilemma. They realize they can't save both the sailor and the ship (and the rest of the people on it). With mournful faces, they reach for the axes and cut the ropes.

At this point in our LDC seminar, I ask, "How much is it costing you to *not* cut the rope(s)?" Not dealing properly with a single team member's behavior often costs you—and your team—more than you realize. Regardless of the person's professional contributions, the behavioral consequence can be (and often is) much greater. Even if the behavioral issue isn't a "ship sinker," it may still be holding back someone on your team, if not the entire team, in some way.

People can improve and grow in their behavior patterns if they are open to correction and advice; sometimes it only takes one person telling the truth to open someone's eyes and set him or her on a better path. Leaders have the responsibility to provide intentional help and encouragement in behavior that affects a person's job and the team.

Skills

The third development essential is skills. This is the easiest of the three to work on, but it's still very important and often overlooked or assumed.

We frequently hear the word "competent" (or its opposite, "incompetent") in connection with leadership. But how does a leader lead with competence?

First and foremost, competence means making good decisions. But how do we do *that*? What skills must we exercise to be good decision-makers?

Consider the arena of childrearing. Being an effective parent is a great and noble goal, but how is it achieved? What skills are necessary to carry out the responsibility of parenting successfully? We tend to assume that if the vision is clear, the needed skills will surface automatically. Although some skills may be innate and instinctual to pick up, most are learned.

I was attending a workshop at a business conference. Members of the audience were milling around the room. Various conversations were underway. Finally, the emcee came into the room and approached the lectern. I remember thinking to myself, "Oh, great, I'm glad we're starting." I was really looking forward to hearing the workshop presenter on his topic.

As I turned my gaze upon the emcee, I quickly realized there was going to be a problem. The young professional had an uncertain look on his face as he looked out across the room, still buzzing with conversation and activity. He hesitantly cleared his throat, then softly and without conviction spoke into the microphone: "OK, can we get started?" The pockets of chatter and laughter continued. His eyes darted around the room. "Excuse me," he stammered. He began knocking on the wooden lectern with increasing vigor to try to get everyone's attention. I wasn't sure he was going to pull everyone together. Finally, he did secure enough people's attention to bring order and proceed in getting the workshop started.

Starting a meeting effectively is a simple skill, one that most of us would assume anyone could do. Yet, because this leader was not competent in this one important area, his presentation got off to a poor beginning. Later, I was asked to provide leadership coaching to this professional, and we started with this simple skill.

Next Steps: Asking Questions about the Development Essentials

To help identify possible development areas, we recommend applying some specific questions to the three development essentials (thinking, behavior, and skills). Make a practice of asking these questions about those you lead:

1. What do they need to be successful/effective in what they are responsible for?

- What new or expanded *thinking* is critical for this role?
- What conduct, actions, or reactions *(behavior)* are needed?
- Which specific *skills* do they need for the role?

2. What do *you* see in them? As a coach, supervisor, or parent, you have a unique vantage point to observe those you lead by looking through the lenses of thinking, behavior, and skills.

3. What do *they* see in themselves? I often ask, "As you think about this responsibility and what it takes to do it well, is there an area or two you'd like to get some more training/development in?"

4. What are others seeing? Teammates, colleagues, friends, and family can see things we are often blinded to. What might be obvious to others we either can't or won't see or acknowledge. Without becoming aware of our blind spots and listening to others, we may miss out on much-needed development.

Development Discovery with the "W.I.N."

Coaching conversations can be very helpful for development. Following are three questions that can foster dialogue about development opportunities and needs. Whereas the previous section offered questions that can be asked anytime, these questions (represented by the acronym W.I.N.) are good during reflection on past experiences and looking ahead to experiences to come.

W—What Went Well?
Development shouldn't center only on problem areas. It's important also to look for areas of strength or accomplishment. This question brings out those positive aspects. Perhaps an event revealed an area of giftedness, but that gift is still in embryonic form and can become an area of development focus moving forward.

I—What Needs Improvement?
We tend to be cognizant of the things we could/need to do better. Still, we may be tempted to sweep them under the rug or bury them (some-

times out of embarrassment or an unwillingness to name our shortcomings). Identifying specific improvement areas is critical to future success.

N—What Are the Next Steps?

To move from discovery to actual development requires action. Knowing what is needed to get to a destination is important, but it's not the same as actually starting the journey to get there. What will be your first practical steps in this odyssey?

Discover is both an obvious and (often) assumed Operational Aspect. To Develop well, a leader needs an intentional, thoughtful process of discovery, along with good observation and specificity, to pinpoint how and in what areas to develop those they lead.

Chapter 9 Key Takeaways:

- Development cannot be assumed to occur due to experience or completion of some omnibus "development workshops"; it takes intentionality and specificity.
- Three development essentials are thinking, behavior, and skills.
- Thinking can be a major development barrier; developing one's thinking can be powerful, however, since everything we say and do flows from our thoughts.
- Use a variety of questions (as recommended in this chapter) to determine specific areas of thinking, behaviors, and skills that need to be developed.

Chapter 10
Develop Operational Aspect #2: Teach

A large international service agency was experiencing what had become its norm: a significant number of staff members leaving each year after only a relatively short time in the field. So much work to learn a new language, so much effort and expense to move their families to another country—and all of it seemed like a total waste.

Each of the departing staff members had begun their assignments with eagerness and passion. In addition, the agency's organizational structure appeared solid: regional directors oversaw country leaders, who in turn oversaw city leaders. The chain of command couldn't be clearer. Furthermore, the higher-up leaders seemed to be people of real capacity and commitment. When I asked these leaders how they felt about those they led, they expressed a heart for those who reported to them and sadness over each exodus.

What was going on? My team and I conducted some exit interviews and uncovered a pattern in the responses: People were leaving because of poor experiences with their supervisors. This was painful for the leaders to hear. Not only did they genuinely care for those for whom they were responsible, but each leader was deeply committed to setting a great example for those on their team. They worked hard, putting in long hours to fulfill the agency of their mission. They communicated their availability to their direct reports, whom they encouraged to call or message them anytime.

In short, these leaders were working hard already; exhorting them to try harder or care more wasn't the answer. An increase in effort wasn't what was needed. Instead, they needed to better channel that effort. For leaders to develop, and for them to develop those under them, they need to infuse new information into their people and their work; old thinking needs to be challenged and replaced with new thinking. In other words, leaders need to teach—as well as be taught themselves.

Passing on Information

For people to grow and develop, they need input. Real, pertinent information provokes change in people's lives—especially when that information challenges existing paradigms.

Our paradigms form the basis for how we see the world. Paradigms are frameworks of our basic assumptions and ways of thinking—lenses through which we perceive reality. And we all have them. Yet, our paradigms not only inform us; they can also limit us.

When Sherry and I married in 1973, I was amazed at how different her thinking was from mine. Our male-female, Texas-Virginia, extrovert-introvert, romantic-stoic differences were startling and challenging. We had different paradigms for our lives. Initially, we each fought to hang onto our own frameworks. After all, that is how we had always perceived reality. Our understanding of how life and relationships work was based on what we knew—previous information stored away, mostly unconsciously.

I can remember going to our first marriage weekend retreat led by a couple much further down the road than we were. They taught principles and practices that were new to both of us. This new information challenged both of our paradigms. I vividly recall sitting there, taking notes, and thinking to myself, "Wow, I didn't know all this! So, that's why Sherry asks the questions she does!" The new information we gleaned at that retreat enabled each of us to *understand and build on* our differences rather than to *defend* our differences. We could *complement* each other rather than *compete* with each other. We learned information that enabled us to change and begin relating differently.

The Necessity of Continuing Education

We all have and live according to certain information, but that information is incomplete. We aren't so much ignorant as limited. When coaching leaders, one of the phrases I use most often is, "Let's think about that for a moment." What I'm saying, in essence, is "OK, what you're telling me is based on what you know. Let's examine that, build on it, and see if you can understand the situation from a different perspective. That expanded viewpoint will be a benefit to you, enabling you to be an even better leader."

No one is a blank slate; everyone knows *something*. However, no one ever gets to the point of knowing all they ever need to know. In addition, even for those considered experts or veterans, new information is always being created and uncovered. Thus, continuing education is a necessity for all people, no matter where they stand in an organization.

With the large international agency mentioned in the vignette that opened this chapter, we began to teach its leaders a new way of looking at their leadership responsibility. Those leaders wanted to lead well, but their staff would continue to resign until their paradigm shifted.

Previously, these higher-level leaders were spending about 95 percent of their time, energy, and focus on their own local work. While that pattern may have provided a good example of what the agency's mission was all about, it left disproportionately little time and energy for leading, developing, and caring for those throughout their region for whom they were responsible. To address this problem, we helped rewrite these leaders' job descriptions based on our leadership model. The change was drastic but necessary. Given the number of staff each leader was in charge of leading and how dispersed they were geographically, the regional leaders were now asked to spend a minimum of 70 percent of their time on leadership responsibilities; their own local work, by contrast, had to be cut back to only 30 percent of their time.

This adjustment was a shock to the leaders at first—it was new, different, and a challenge to their existing paradigm. But it was necessary for creating the space in their schedules that would allow them to lead *all* of their staff well throughout the regions they each oversaw.

This paradigm shift incorporated our teaching, and it turned the organization around. Since then, the agency has seen not only a significant drop in staff turnover but an increase in overall staff satisfaction and productivity measures.

Learning and Sharing New Information

Part of your strategy as a developmental leader must include exposing your people to fresh ideas. In a workplace setting, this requires you to stay up to speed, even ahead of the curve, in your own field so you can share new insights with those you lead. (In a family setting, this includes slowly introducing your children to new aspects of the world, at a level and pace appropriate to their age.)

In addition to passing along new knowledge, it's important to encourage those you lead to be proactive themselves in staying aware of the happenings that relate to their jobs and fields. Be open to hearing the new ideas they run across and invite them to share those ideas with you and the rest of the team.

As I've mentioned earlier, I once had the privilege of serving as the national collegiate director (for the United States) of an international corporation. In my role, I met one day with a leader from one of our sister organizations. Tyler was in a similar type of work, but he was not a competitor so much as a fellow colleague in the same area of service. Our lunch meeting therefore had a collegial feel to it (something that, admittedly, is not always realistic in different situations).

Over lunch I asked Tyler if he thought he could set up a meeting between me and his national director, who was headquartered in another state. When he asked the nature of this desired visit, I shared that I'd like to learn how my counterpart views his role and what he has learned about how to be even more effective in his work, which is so similar to mine.

My lunchmate asked, "Why would you be interested in that?"

I responded, "Well, I've been with my organization for twenty-five years now. I know how we think and what we're working on. I don't need more of the same. To move us forward, I think I need some fresh ideas and perspectives. I've always admired the work your group does. I know I can learn a lot from interacting with your leaders."

Tyler seemed intrigued if a bit surprised. After a pause, I prodded, "So, do you think you could set up the meeting for me?"

He did, and I wound up learning tons of new information and ideas from that other national director. Some of those learnings are incorporated into our work to this day.

The encouraging thing about this Operational Aspect of teaching is that everyone can learn. And, in fact, everyone *needs* to keep learning. We only need a willingness to do so.

Winston Churchill is quoted as saying, "I am always ready to learn, although I do not always like being taught."[24] It can be just as true that leaders do not always like teaching. Some even feel inadequate for the task, wondering, "Who am I to teach others?" Both attitudes—not wanting to learn and not wanting to teach—hinder your ability to develop others.

It's important to remind the person you see in the mirror each morning of two things:

1. You have never surpassed the stage of not needing to be taught. Leaders are learners (or should be!). This lifelong capacity to learn is a wonderful aspect of the human mind and spirit!
2. You as a leader have the privilege and responsibility to teach others. Those you lead expect and need you to teach them. Effective teaching enables your people to grow in competence and confidence. Without teaching, we consign those we lead to stagnation, opening them up to a higher likelihood of making mistakes that could have been avoided and of performing below their potential.

Chapter 10 Key Takeaways:

- Teaching people involves challenging their paradigms—the frameworks by which they see life.
- Leaders are both learners themselves in addition to teachers. This process of learning is lifelong and shared between leaders and those they lead.
- All leaders have a responsibility to share new information (teach) those they lead; neglecting this role leads to stagnation and diminished contributions among their people.

---

24 From a speech in the House of Commons (delivered November 4, 1952); the quote was later printed in *The Observer* (a British newspaper).

Chapter 11
Develop Operational Aspect #3: Model

"Let's go for a walk," I said to Doug, beckoning him to the door. Soon, we were ambling along the seashore near Dublin, Ireland, talking through the day we had just spent meeting one by one with his direct reports.

Doug had been introduced to the LDC Leadership Model at one of our seminars. Among the most intelligent leaders I'd ever been around (sometimes I had to sneak a peek at my dictionary app to look up a word he used), I knew he understood our model very well conceptually. However, with this visit—seeing him in his element—I could see how well he understood (and was putting into practice) the model experientially.

I had given Doug some specific action items for employing our model based on what I knew of his situation. One was a Set Direction exercise. The other was simply a recommendation to develop his team members by giving them certain information they needed. He was to do both of these things in one-on-one appointments with each of them, while I sat in as an observer.

As we went from appointment to appointment, I watched Doug while he watched his direct reports. Now, walking along and processing what we'd each observed, it was rewarding to see him pause and respond to questions I asked with comments such as, "Oh, so that's what setting direction means."

Asking Doug to implement certain elements of our model in live leadership situations with real people, and then taking time to process those experiences through a mutual exchange of questions and comments, allowed for a level of learning and training that can't happen in a classroom/seminar setting. As Doug engaged the model in his own context, the light bulb was going off for him. Conceptual knowledge was being solidified with experiential understanding. And experiential understanding was enabled because my questions and feedback were based not solely on his perception of what happened (a limitation of virtual coaching) but on my firsthand observations (not filtered through his own interpretation). For Doug to "get it," he needed my eyes, my perspective, and my time, not merely my questions.

Modeling is about observing, seeing, and watching. It goes beyond merely hearing or reading. It's not a one-way activity, either, but a two-way one. In its simplest form, modeling involves two components: (1) you watch me and (2) I watch you. This approach to learning and training is also known as apprenticeship—a concept much more familiar to people hundreds of years ago than to people today. In modern times, we tend to refer to the apprenticeship idea as "on-the-job training." In earlier times, modeling and apprenticeship was the primary way people prepared for a career: by observing a more experienced worker in the field, and by jumping in and working alongside him or her.

You Watch Me

As learners, we need information (see chapter 10). We also need example. This vital method of learning and growing can be seen at a very early age. One of the basic tenets of child development is imitation. Children watch and imitate what they see even before they are capable of cognitively understanding what they see or how it's done. (Think of the child who hilariously repeats a grown-up phrase before he or she truly comprehends the words or meaning!)

Imitation is also integral to leadership. We observe leaders in our own lives from the time we're young. First, it's parents, then teachers and coaches. For better or for worse, we may also imitate admired public figures in sports, entertainment, industry, and politics. Whether their examples are good or bad (or, as in most cases, a mixture of the two), all of these people shape our concepts of what those in positions of leadership and authority think, say, and do. We have thousands of images stored away in the recesses of our minds that form a leadership concept collage within us. These models, and their collective impression on us, are powerful. For many in my generation, this collage comprises images like the rugged John Wayne, the charismatic John F. Kennedy, and the courageous early astronauts.

We all need examples. To illustrate this in our leadership seminars, I show a slide of a master cobbler. The old shoemaker is sitting on his cobbler's bench working on a shoe. Close at his side is a young lad, the apprentice, who likewise is seated on a cobbler's bench, working on another shoe. The picture depicts the important practice of modeling and observing. The master has undoubtedly told the cobbler-in-training how to work the heel of the shoe, for instance. By sitting next to the experienced cobbler as he does the same, the young apprentice can watch how the master works the heel *in practice*.

We often underestimate the power of letting others watch us as the pacesetter in the area in which we want them to develop and progress. But sometimes, this form of developing those we lead is more powerful than any lecture or briefing we can give.

An Example from Literature

Even if you've never read the Bible, you've probably heard the story of David and Goliath. A young lad, with just a sling and some stones, slays a mighty giant. Described in the book of 1 Samuel, this story has become the proof text for cheering on the "little guy" against the "big guy." But have you ever looked closely at the text (1 Samuel 17) to read of the aftermath of David's action? His victory had a larger impact than merely taking down a single behemoth.

Let me set the scene for you: King Saul and his army are facing off against the Philistine army, which includes a giant named Goliath. This Goliath is a pretty big dude ("six cubits and a span," 1 Samuel 17:4 says, which equates to over nine feet tall!). One army stands on a mountain on one side of a valley, the other army on a mountain on the other side. For forty days, Goliath comes out and challenges Saul's army to a man-to-man fight.

Saul and his army are glued to their hillside, paralyzed with fear (1 Samuel 17:11, 24). Instead of facing this menace himself, the leader Saul stays behind the lines trying to bribe someone to do it in his place. As the story goes, a young shepherd boy named David comes upon the scene to bring supplies to his brothers. He hears Goliath's challenge and mockery. He decides to do something. Going to King Saul, he essentially proclaims, "Never fear, David is here" (my paraphrase). This is either one brave shepherd or a crazy boy!

After some back-and-forth with King Saul, David is finally allowed to go out to meet Goliath with his sling and five smooth stones. He takes down the giant on his first toss (1 Samuel 17:49). Then an amazing thing happens. The text tells us that "the men of Judah and Israel rose with a shout and pursued the Philistines" (1 Samuel 17:52).

"Wait a minute," you might be asking. "What unglued Saul's army from their hillside?" After being immobilized with fear for almost six weeks, they're now seen chasing the fleeing Philistine army. What released the warrior in each of them?

They saw a giant-killer.

The Israelites did not need a seminar on how to throw a spear or fight with a sword. This was an experienced army, and its soldiers knew how to wage war. Information on techniques was not the need. They needed a model, an example. Observing David released them from their doubts and fears to do what they already knew how to do.

I Watch You

In the master cobbler and his apprentice picture previously mentioned, there's a second dynamic at play besides the youngster watching the more experienced shoemaker. The master cobbler, by sitting side by side with his apprentice, can also observe the apprentice. How well is he learning the trade? Where does he need additional guidance or correction? Both dynamics—"you watch me" and "I watch you"—are necessary.

As seen in my time with Doug (from the opening vignette of this chapter), there is a vast difference between cognitive knowledge and experiential understanding. Misunderstandings can easily occur among those we lead if we're never present to observe them "in action." The young cobbler may think he has the process of working a shoe heel down pat, but only when the master sees what the apprentice is doing firsthand can he notice a critical error—perhaps a subtle one that the apprentice could not have discerned himself. By being there and watching those we lead, we have the benefit of firsthand rather than secondhand information that's filtered through others' viewpoints.

Why Two-Way Modeling Is Often Lacking

The benefits of modeling may seem obvious, and yet, the "you watch me/I watch you" approach is often sorely lacking in leadership development today. I believe four reasons, or mistakes, explain this deficiency. As I discuss each, I think you'll see why these mistakes can actually harm a leader's ability to effectively execute *all three* Primary Responsibilities (Lead, Develop, and Care).

Mistake #1: We equate information assimilation with training.

In chapter 3, I mentioned my brother teaching his students how to juggle. That story perfectly illustrates this mistake. Knowing information about how to juggle did not mean the students could actually juggle if they were handed several balls. Training involves not only information dissemination (teaching) but also experience with observation (modeling) and feedback (coaching). We'll discuss the third component (coaching) in the next chapter. For now, know that it's critical for leaders to go beyond simply distributing information. An instruction booklet, or even a lecture, simply doesn't cut it; an instruction booklet plus an example of someone enacting those instructions is far superior.

One leader I was coaching pushed back a bit on this idea. He said he gets most of his instruction on the internet and doesn't need a real-life person as an example. When I asked where exactly he got his instruction, he mentioned YouTube. In actuality, once I saw the types of videos he was viewing, I realized he was pushing back unnecessarily. He *was* going beyond instructions. He was simply gleaning his content from a *recorded model*. In some cases, such an example may not suffice, and physical presence may be necessary. But for what he was learning, the YouTube model was serving the purpose—allowing observation of an example.

Mistake #2: We substitute reports for presence.

Leaders often request reports—on progress, production, expenditures, employee morale, and so on. These writeups detail how things are going under their leadership.

To be sure, reports have their place. We need information on what's taking place at the ground level, and our direct reports are often the best ones to supply it. Requesting data and updates from those we lead is a way to keep our finger on the pulse of how the work is going without micromanaging. (After all, few things stifle workflow more than a boss who can't let go of the steering wheel!)

However, an over-reliance on reports can be costly. This is especially true when assessing people and relationships, because numbers alone can't tell the whole story in an area so subjective. But even in areas that lend themselves to numeric evaluation, it's important to remember that the interpretation of numbers can be subjective—filtered through a particular lens. What is reported or interpreted may be completely true, but it may also be a partial picture.

I was sitting in on an executive team meeting of a client. The team members were reviewing status reports on progress toward their company's mission. These regional leaders each had a dispersed field representing several countries. I listened without saying anything for over an hour. Finally, one of the leaders looked at me and said, "You haven't made any comments. Do you have any observations?"

"Yes, I do," I replied. "How would you like to hear it: straight or sugar-coated?"

"Give it to us straight," he responded.

"Well, it's been my experience that organizations that rely heavily upon reports do so because they don't really know what's going on in their areas of responsibility," I explained. "The reports give the illusion they do know what's going on."

The team members sat in silence, unsure how to respond. Finally, one person asked me, "Isn't there a place for reports?"

"Yes, of course," I told them, but then went on to qualify my answer. "Reports," I explained, "are valuable in that they provide a platform for asking questions, and for knowing where to follow up and probe further. But reports by themselves aren't enough because they don't usually tell the full story, including the organizational health and tone of the company. Many of the intangibles, like attitude and real growth and development of the staff, simply don't show up on reports. The numbers may look good on one report, and yet the key players may leave the company before the next one is even on the table."

The point is that we can get so busy (or, in some cases, so lazy) that we begin to rely heavily if not exclusively on what we read from writeups of our direct reports. We need to pair such updates with our presence—getting into the department or out in the field to watch and observe for ourselves. Otherwise, all that we're modeling is how to receive and process reports.

Mistake #3: We substitute virtual presence for actual presence.

This mistake should be qualified. Virtual presence is a wonderful option we have today thanks to modern technology, and in many ways, it allows leaders to stay in closer touch with those they lead than was ever possible in the past. Yet, virtual presence (e.g., videoconferencing, voice conference calls, or similar mechanisms) should not be the exclusive means of interaction. There are aspects of in-person presence that no video session can capture. In addition, modeling is difficult to do during occasionally prescribed windows of time, which are often short.

Full disclosure: **LDNGlobal** coaches leaders all over the world, and logistically, we cannot be everywhere even if we all traveled constantly; thus, we use virtual communication modes frequently. I have video chats with our clients' leaders almost every day I'm home. These definitely have their place. Virtual modes of interaction are also much better than snail mail, email, texting, and even voice calls for getting a sense of how a person is doing. Body language and tone—key aspects of nonverbal communication—can be discerned, for example.

Still, there's a danger in using video chatting as an exclusive substitute for face-to-face presence. A high-ranking military officer has been quoted as saying, "Virtual presence is actual absence."[25] The distance that exists geographically has an often-subconscious impact on those we lead, creating a distance relationally and emotionally. Why do you think the President of the United States nearly always makes a point to be present at a military post overseas on major holidays such as Thanksgiving?

Mistake #4: We don't expend the time and resources needed to make modeling (and other aspects of development) possible.

Time and money are limited. Actual presence with our team members can be costly, especially if they're in another country, spread across multiple locations, or on different schedules (e.g., in the case of a hospital staff). And yet, as we've seen, in-person presence is essential and irreplaceable.

---

25   Admiral Mike Mullen, National Defense University, Fort McNair, Washington D.C., August 16, 2005.

Leader development is also costly, often requiring that senior leaders spend precious hours with younger members of their team, modeling for them and teaching them how to do their jobs better. We ask, "Why would we double up on something when one person could do it? Isn't it a better use of resources to divide the work and get more done?" The answer is that these sacrifices of resources are costly in the short term but not in the long term. The lack of genuine development in one leader will cost other leaders, and everyone these leaders lead, later. This principle applies in a less formal setting, too, like a household: a mother modeling for her child how to fold laundry is not nearly as time-efficient as folding the clothes all by herself, but the comparatively small extra time expended early in that child's life can pay off exponentially for her later.

Leader development has to be prioritized *with our resources*, including appropriate adjustments made in the budget and in job descriptions, if it's going to get done. It's not something you simply do if you happen to have some time left over—believe me, you won't! An intentional cutting back of the workload and a reallocation of some funds may be necessary to make room for development; this may require accepting a short-term hit for a long-term gain.

A company in India called Hindustan Unilever had the reputation of being a leader factory—producing a continual stream of effective, quality leaders for the company.[26] The company's bottom line was also doing very well. In researching why this was happening, I noted that upper managers' job descriptions all contained the requirement of dedicating 40 percent of their time to the development of younger leaders. That meant two things. First, 40 percent of what would usually be included in their responsibilities had to be delegated elsewhere to give them the time they needed. Second, instead of a net loss, they were in fact producing a net gain in their multiplication of key leaders. The investment was worth it!

Practical Steps

Leave Your Office

The underlying principle about modeling is that leaders are their own best tools for developing others. What we as leaders know, what we

---

26 Boris Groysberg, *Chasing Stars: The Myth of Talent and the Portability of Performance* (Princeton, NJ: Princeton University Press, 2010).

have learned and experienced, the mistakes we've made, and an awareness of our own strengths and weaknesses all play a strategic role in developing others. The leader who is isolated in the deluxe corner office hunched over a computer screen all day every day with the office door closed forfeits his or her greatest asset in training younger leaders.

Those who invite others to observe them in their leadership context—and who likewise take the time to observe others (future or developing leaders) in their contexts—build for the future.

The importance of getting out of the office was vividly illustrated in a United Airlines television commercial from 1990 called "Speech."[27] It begins with the head of the sales department speaking to his entire sales force that he had received a phone call that morning from one of the airline's oldest customers. The customer informed him that after twenty years of business together, the airline had been fired. The customer said he "didn't know [them] anymore." The head of the department said he knew why: "We used to do business with a handshake, face to face. Now it's a phone call or a fax [this was in 1990, after all]. Then, it's a 'I'll get back to you later with another fax, probably.' Well, folks, something's got to change. That's why we're going to set out on a little face-to-face chat with every customer we have." The sales director begins handing out United tickets to the entire sales force, indicating that the staff members had to leave their office cubicles and show up at the clients' offices.

What was this commercial emphasizing? The important of actual presence. It's worth the time and expense. We can be the most "plugged in" generation and the most "out-of-touch" generation at the same time. But if we substitute our devices for real, live presence, we'll suffer the consequences.

Always Take Someone with You

I rarely travel alone. Whether it's a trip overseas or walking to another part of the office complex, I like to take someone with me. It's part of what I call "leading with a developmental mindset." Get the job done but think of ways for others to be developed in the process—for example, by having them tag along on a business trip (whether it's across the hall

---

27 This United Airlines commercial from 1990, "Speech," is accessible at https://youtu.be/mU2rpcAABbA.

or across an ocean). This tactic helps me be more efficient with my time while developing another person. He or she will sometimes ask, "What do you want to do as we visit that office?" Sometimes I'll ask my companion to contribute something, but usually I simply say, "Oh, just tag along and watch."

My focus on these trips is on my companion's thinking—specifically, his or her capacity to think at a higher level of leadership. Can he shift from thinking mainly within his department to thinking more broadly about the company? At the conclusion of such trips, I ask my companion, "What did you see? If you were the supervisor of that office we visited, what would encourage you? What would concern you? What's working, and where might that office be 'stuck'? As you met that team, who caught your attention as a potential future leader?" I'm helping my companion develop and elevate his thinking.

Such trips aren't merely to develop others, though. They're mutually beneficial. By having another set of eyes and ears with me, I can pick up on more than I would pick up on by myself.

I took one younger colleague, Ellery, to an onsite visit with one of our regional representatives. On our drive back, I asked him what he had observed during the visit. Ellery remarked that he'd noticed some tension between a couple of the team members in that office. I asked him to explain what he saw. As he concluded his explanation, I thanked him and told him I had totally missed his observation. His presence not only gave him exposure to another office, but it enabled me to bring the potential relational issue to the attention of the regional representative overseeing that office. The representative did address the problem and helped the team members work through their differences.

Chapter 11 Key Takeaways:

- Modeling is a two-part responsibility: "you watch me" and "I watch you."
- Four mistakes explain deficiencies in modeling among leaders today: we equate information assimilation with training; we substitute reports for presence; we substitute virtual presence for actual presence; and we don't expend the resources needed to make modeling possible.

- Leaders are their own best tools for developing others; practical steps toward modeling include leaving your office (without doing so, it's hard to achieve the two-way modeling approach), and taking someone along with you when you do.

Chapter 12
Develop Operational Aspect #4: Coach

Some colleagues and I were talking one day about some of the legendary coaches in sports: Bear Bryant, Woody Hayes, and Nick Saban (on the collegiate football front), as well as John Wooden, Dean Smith, Pat Summitt, and Mike Krzyzewski (collegiate basketball), among others. As we talked, we noticed that much of the basis of our unscientific analysis of the best coaches centered on their winning records—the number of games and national championships each had won.

Certainly, wins are an outcome of great athletic coaching. A coach with a losing record simply doesn't make a list of greats. Yet, we found ourselves beginning to question our own basis for assessment. Those coaches mentioned were undoubtedly some of the greatest coaches of their era. Their winning records offered proof of that fact. But was there something more to their greatness than their win/loss records? What's the real mark of a great coach? Does great coaching achieve something bigger and better than a quantity of wins or national championships?

A few years ago, my colleague Henry Clay was attending one of his high school reunions when he ran into his old basketball coach. After reminding Coach Saunders of who he was, he added, "I wasn't one of your better players." Boy, was that ever an understatement (by Henry's own admission)! Henry had gone out for basketball because he loved shooting baskets and playing one-on-one pick-up games with friends. But frankly, as soon as he was on a court with nine other people running around, he felt (and looked) lost. So, he spent most of the season on the bench. Only once did he get to dress out for a game (and that was only because so many on his team were out sick at the same time).

When Coach Saunders encountered Henry all those decades later, it was unclear how much of his former player's sad, short career in basketball he would even remember. But the old coach took Henry by surprise when *he responded, "If I'd been a better coach, you'd have been a better player." "His comment blew me away," Henry told me later.*

Whether the coach was right or not wasn't the point; for him to view his responsibility as coach in the way he did left my friend deeply moved, and Henry never forgot that conversation. As we talked about it, it hit us that Henry's coach's admission was really what great coaching is all about— namely, helping others improve and be better (players, workers, students, or whatever) than before.

The Critical Need for Coaching

Teaching and modeling are never enough in the developmental process. I was attending a workshop on leader development that was conducted by Professor Howard Hendricks of Dallas Theological Seminary when he made a rather surprising statement. This teacher of five decades said that "teaching without coaching is a waste of time." There were few of the same caliber as Dr. Hendricks, who had an amazing ability to teach well. Yet, he was saying that without feedback and new input, preferably from an experienced and knowledgeable in-person observer, improvement is generally lacking.

Early in my teaching career, I remember a veteran teacher remarking that some teachers are in their twentieth year of teaching while others are in their first year of teaching for the twentieth time. The difference? No improvement. Just doing what they have always been doing. This is where coaching comes in.

What Is a Coach?

Whereas teaching is primarily about instruction, and modeling is about observation, coaching is about improvement.

"To coach" comes from an old French word that means "a vehicle to transport a person from one place to another." The word is still used in the transportation industry, as in "to travel (in) coach." Beginning in the nineteenth century, the word coach began to be used to refer to a private tutor who helped students prepare for their examinations. This is the idea of a scholastic coach. In the late 1800s, "coach" began to be used for older experienced athletes who could guide and develop younger athletes, leading them toward improvement and victory—we still have sports coaches to this day (and many of them are indeed former athletes of the sport they coach).

In recent decades, the term has evolved yet again to refer to someone who helps a person advance in his or her personal and professional development. This kind of coach facilitates growth through questions, input, and interaction. At their best, coaches help ordinary people do extraordinary things, reaching a much higher level of performance and contribution than would have been possible by themselves.

At **LDNGlobal**, we say it this way: *You may be good. You may even be better than everyone else. But you will never be as good as you can be without a coach.*

Types of Coaching

There are two main approaches to coaching people in their development: directive and nondirective.

With **directive coaching**, the coach sets the agenda and assignments and assesses against a known model. Directive coaching occurs when a more advanced leader develops a younger leader toward a new leadership position (often within the same organization for which they both work). For example, a project manager might be coached toward a department head role. The coach knows what the new role entails, including the kind of thinking, behavior, and skills required to succeed in that role. The coach creates a "program" of content, assignments, and actions to build certain knowledge into the leader to equip him or her for the aspirational role. We call this approach *coaching to the model.*

Nondirective coaching becomes a more common and helpful approach as time passes in a person's career and life. This kind of coaching works in all kinds of situations, from the employee moving up the leadership ladder to children in the home who are growing up and taking on more responsibility. With nondirective coaching, the coachee (rather than the coach) determines more of the agenda; that is, the one coached decides how he/she wants or needs to improve and takes steps to do so. In essence, the person being coached is taking more of the initiative and saying, "I'm in this role, and I'd like to learn how to do this aspect of it better." The coach's part is to ask good questions and give minimal input, allowing the coachee to draw upon his or her own reserve of knowledge and experience. The coach is less proactive, more reactive. We call this approach *coaching to the need*.

As you seek to coach your people in their development, it is important to discern how and when you should be directive or nondirective in your coaching. Sometimes, giving suggestions and input is needed and appropriate; other times, your people will develop best if you ask them good questions and place the onus of improvement on them. As a leader, you should develop your skills with both approaches, because neither directive nor nondirective coaching is *always* better. Each approach is useful depending on the person you're coaching and the circumstance. Whatever approach you're using, it behooves you to focus on "being a better coach" (as my colleague's former high school basketball coach realized he should have done), knowing this will naturally help your people become "better players."

You don't have to coach perfectly—no one ever does. But you *should* show a genuine interest in your people's growth (what you can give them), not just in their contributions (what they can give you), as this *care* for their *development* will communicate volumes to them.

The Importance of Actual Presence

As in the case of modeling (focused on observation), the best coaching demands your actual presence (not just virtual presence) with your people from time to time. Let me illustrate from a personal experience.

In one of my national leadership roles, I introduced a new initiative to my regional directors one day. When I got home that night, my wife, Sherry, asked me how the presentation went.

"It went really well," I told her. "Everyone seemed to agree with it."

Now Sherry knows me well, so she followed with, "What pushback was there?"

I proudly announced that there wasn't any, to which she responded, "Why do you think there wasn't any pushback?"

"Because it's a great idea … and I presented it well," I said with a somewhat sheepish smile.

Sherry had only one comment in reply: "I think you need to ask them why they didn't push back."

She was right. And so, after initial reluctance, I agreed to ask them the next day.

Before I tell you what happened the next day, though, let me interject a hypothetical situation. If I had called my leadership coach Mike (who lives across the country) that same night, the conversation probably would have gone quite differently. He'd likely have heard my enthusiastic report—how no one questioned the need for the initiative—and said something like, "That's great, Terry! You must have presented it brilliantly! Keep up the good leadership." See, Mike doesn't know me like my wife does, nor was he present in the meeting to get a realistic, unfiltered picture of what happened. Mike's affirmation would've been misguided, without either of us realizing it. (We'll come back to Mike in a moment.)

Now, for the end of the story: The next morning, as my regional directors gathered for another day of meetings together, I led with what I'd promised my wife to say: "No one pushed back at all after I presented the new initiative yesterday. What do you honestly think about it? What questions or concerns do you have?" I immediately knew I was in trouble as they all started looking at each other and squirming in their seats, as if trying to decide, "Who's going to tell him?"

Finally, Dan summoned up enough courage to say, "The reason we didn't push back is that we have come to realize that when you are excited about an idea, you are going to do it regardless of what we say. You've already made up your mind. We cannot out-argue you, and the reality is that we are just tired of trying."

Ouch. The truth can hurt the worst when we most need to hear it. And I needed to hear this. Rather than getting a virtual pat on the back for good leadership, I got just the opposite.

Now, back to Mike for a moment. Let's suppose my leadership coach, instead of being across the country connecting via a video chat, had been sitting in the initial presentation in person. What would he have seen that I totally missed? He would have looked around and noticed that the further I got into the presentation, the more shut-down the team was becoming. He would have caught the nonverbal cues the team verbally broadcasted the following day (at my invitation). He would have seen the attempts to interject their own comments or questions of which I was totally ignorant due to being so caught up in my own momentum. Instead of assuming it was a great job of leading, he would have seen firsthand the terrible job of leading I was actually doing. Instead of leading my team members, I was bulldozing them!

The downside of virtual coaching is that the information the coach receives is filtered through the lens of the person being coached. Even though the people being coached may not be *trying* to hide anything, it's human nature to see what we want to see and to ignore what we don't want to see. A virtual coach can only respond to the viewpoint of the coached—making his or her perspective limited in helpfulness.

You Can't Coach Everyone

Years ago, I had the opportunity to attend some football practices when the legendary Paul "Bear" Bryant was head coach at the University of Alabama. What first caught my attention as I walked out onto the practice field was the beehive of activity. There were more than 175 players and upwards of 20 coaches scattered over several practice fields all running drills. It was a three-ring circus of movement.

I planted myself under the Bear's shadow, situated right in the middle of this cacophony of noise and movement. Occasionally, I'd hear him through his bullhorn barking out comments directed toward one cluster of players and coaches.

As I walked off the field at the end of the practice, I asked one of the coaches, Louis Campbell (a good friend of mine), "How in the world can Coach Bryant coach that many players? I never realized there were so many players at a practice. How does he do it?"

"Oh, he doesn't coach the players," my friend responded. "He coaches the coaches. Each coach has a practice routine he is to follow. Coach Bryant is watching to see how well each coach is doing with that role.

By teaching us ahead of the practice what we're to be doing with our individual responsibilities and then being with us as we execute, he multiplies who he is and what he knows through us. We bring who we are and what we know to the practices, of course. But his teaching, observing, and coaching take us to a whole new level of effectiveness. We learn from his observations of being with us."

Coach Bryant's exemplary coaching and two-way modeling were time- and labor-intensive. He wisely recognized that he couldn't coach everyone; there was no feasible way. So, he selectively chose to coach and model for the other coaches. His tactic was extremely effective, and not only was he a different kind of a leader because of it, but he shaped other leaders of the same kind.

You can't be everywhere or everything to everybody. Learning and recognizing your limitations is, as Coach Bryant's example shows, extremely important to your success as a leader.

Practical Steps

Part III contains two acrostic tools, COACH and DRESSCODES, to help you develop your nondirective coaching skills. Many other guides and tools for nondirective coaching exist as well. One approach is to meet with your coachee and start with an open question like, "How would you like to use our time together today?" or "What is the major challenge you're facing right now?" Then, draw out the person, finding out what he or she has tried and thought about already. The goal is to coach/lead the person into coming up with a new plan and examining what obstacles might need to be overcome. Finish your time together by reviewing key takeaways as well as commitments of things the person will do before the next session.

To lead well, coaching is not optional; it's foundational. And when coaching is done in concert with teaching and modeling, the development of those you lead will be well-rounded, with powerful results.

Chapter 12 Key Takeaways:

- Coaching, the final Operational Aspect of Develop, is all about improvement, and everyone (no matter how good they are in a certain area) can stand to improve.
- There are two main approaches to coaching: directive (the coach sets the agenda, coaching toward the model) and indirective (the coached sets the agenda, being coached within the model).
- Coaching requires actual presence to be truly effective.
- A coach has to be selective in who he or she coaches; coaching other coaches will lead to a deeper impact that is then multiplied by others.

The LDC model integrates interrelated actions, which should be combined and carried out with intentionality, undergirded by a shepherd's heart for the people you lead.

Develop: Operational Aspect Summary

Healthy people are growing people. Leading with a developmental mindset means fostering an atmosphere of "always springtime" with yourself and those you lead. Continual, lifelong learning has never been more important than in today's world of rapid change. Yet, Develop is typically the most neglected part of leadership. Its four
Operational Aspects—**Discover, Teach, Model,** and **Coach**—are powerful when combined, unlocking untapped potential. Growth in thinking, behavior, and skills positions people to succeed and continually improve, which in turn benefits those with whom they work and live. Without growth, there is stagnation and a lack of energy. Ideally, Development is done on the go; it's woven into your everyday mindset, and thus you always have time for it.

In Action

Frank had been the human resources director at his company for about five years. During that time, he had often heard leaders complain that they were placed in their roles with little or no training in how to do their jobs. "Sink or swim" seemed to be the prevailing pattern. Now that Frank was being promoted and Mary would succeed him as the new human resources director, he was determined to provide the training that was so often lacking during these transitions. He carefully thought through what information would be helpful to Mary, and in the three months before she replaced him, he met with her several times. He even included her in the meetings she would eventually lead, inviting her to both participate and observe. These activities covered Discover, Teach, and Model; next he would Coach her as she took on her new role. He scheduled a monthly call with her in the first four months of her new position—plus made himself available outside of those times as needed. Afterward, Mary commented that she had never had such a smooth transition to a new job.

Chapter 13
Care Operational Aspect #1: Know

"Know well the condition of your flock and give careful attention to your herds" (Proverbs 27:23). I shared the principle of this ancient proverb with a group of business leaders one day. The proverb especially struck Don, a supervisor at a local business who proceeded to share the lesson he'd learned from a recent, painful experience.

Don had measured the health of his department merely by counting bodies present and watching to make sure those employees were busy. If everyone was there, not in tears or yelling at someone, and appeared to be engaged with their work, he assumed everyone was doing fine.

That perspective had been challenged when one of his newer employees, Michelle, began to be consistently fifteen minutes late for work. Instead of first exploring what might be causing her to be late, he strongly admonished her about the need to be on time. She promised to try to do better. However, the tardiness continued.

Finally, one morning, Michelle's lateness collided with Don's growing impatience. He erupted and publicly fired her, thinking it would be a good lesson to everyone about the importance of his office standards.

After Michelle left the office in humiliation and tears, one of her officemates shared with Don the reason for her pattern of being late. The reason was that she had recently gone through a divorce and, as a single mom with a "deadbeat former husband," she had had to take on another job as a waitress to make ends meet. Her second job was after this job and wasn't finished until almost midnight. The late nights were taking their toll, resulting in her tardiness each morning.

Realizing the mistake he had made in not investigating the situation more, Don called Michelle immediately and asked her to return to the office. When she arrived, he publicly apologized to her (because his firing had been public) for not making the effort to understand what she was facing. He asked her to stay and, because she was a hard-working employee with skill in a critically needed area, he expedited an already-planned increase in her salary, enabling her to drop the second job. It was a painful but profound lesson for him on his responsibility to know more about the condition of his team beyond simply observing whether employees were showing up. In fact, the experience was a turning point in his leadership. As a middle manager, he became more keenly aware that productivity and structure are part of only one side of the coin; the other side entails remembering that he is dealing with real people in real life with real issues that have a real influence on them.

Real People with Real Lives

You can't care well for someone if you don't know—and act on—important realities about them and their lives. That is why Know is the starting point of putting the Primary Responsibility of Care into action.

When you, as a leader, take time to know your people—whether it's direct reports at work, the players of a team you coach, or your own children—you let them know they're valued. Many people feel invisible and unimportant to their leaders—except when the leaders need something from them. Leaders can place such an emphasis on tasks at hand that the people helping them accomplish those tasks come to feel like little more than pawns—means to an end. When leaders make a point of (appropriately) getting to know their people, *just because* (and not for any ulterior motives), the response is usually surprise and appreciation.

This aspect of Know is a tricky one, though. What is appropriate? What should you know, and what is none of your business?

To grow in this area, don't start with the boundaries (those will come in time). Instead, start with understanding how your own thinking limits you from expressing care.

They're Not You

This first consideration is so obvious that we often dismiss it rather than thinking through the implications. The people you lead are not exactly like you. They don't think, feel, or act the same way you do. They don't have the same paradigms or background you have. And their insecurities and anxieties differ from the ones that challenge you. In general, the way others look at life is foreign to you, at least to some degree, and sometimes to a major degree.

Gary Chapman, in his classic book *The Five Love Languages*, discusses how knowing the five basic ways love is understood and expressed is instructional for a spousal relationship (as well as other relationships). Understanding that your significant other may have a different "love language" than yours, and then acting accordingly, is transformational for the relationship. The same applies in a leadership relationship. Those you lead may all work for the same company, be on the same sports team, or come from the same family. Yet, each person is a different creature from you and from each other. As you seek to know each person you lead better, you may explore facts about their:

- Gifts and abilities
- Likes and dislikes
- History and family background
- General life situation/stage
- Stresses they're under at home
- Goals and areas in which they would like to develop

As an exercise, write down a list of the facts you would like *your* supervisor to know and be aware of about *you*. Also, write down how it would make you feel if your leader took the initiative to know and remember those things about you. This will begin to give you a greater sense of what your people would like you to know about them—and how that would make them feel.

Below are just a few of the big areas in which people differ from each other and that are important to consider as you lead.

Personalities and Preferences

Marriages, families, teams, organizations, and companies all have a disparate compilation of personalities, preferences, gifts, and abilities. We all have our likes and dislikes. I still find it hard to believe that some people do not like coconut pie (my favorite!). To be effective, trusted leaders, we need to recognize and appreciate differences. The chart below lists just a few, but keep in mind, these categories aren't hard and fast—rather, they represent ends of spectrums. Each person is a unique combination of these (and other) preferences and tendencies.

Extrovert	Introvert
Thinking	Feeling
Judging	Perceiving
Romantic	Stoic
Early bird	Night owl
Into the details	Concerned with broad principles
Likes to work individually	Likes to work collaboratively
Likes to be alone	Likes to be together with others
Adventurous/risk-taking	Cautious
Proactive (initiator)	Reactive (responder)
Leader	Follower
Watching	Reading

My editor, Jenny, was sharing how she is a high C in the DiSC profile (C = conscientiousness) and a former boss of hers was a high D (D = dominance). The boss hated all the detailed emails that Jenny would send (and thus never read them), and Jenny hated that her boss wouldn't read her emails carefully (this felt disrespectful and careless to her). After taking the DiSC test, Jenny started to see how neither one of them was right or wrong—they just had different communication styles and expectations. The two came to agreement that Jenny would put the most important info in the first sentence of her message. Any other crucial information, she could bold (but with no guarantee it would be read). The rest was optional for her boss to read—but Jenny felt better that the details were there, in writing, in case they were needed.

There are many personality assessment tools available. In addition to the DiSC personality profile assessment, other popular ones include the Myers-Briggs Type Indicator, the Birkman Method (behavioral and occupational assessments), and the Enneagram of Personality test. Any assessment tool must come with a caution: there's a danger in these tools in that they can put people into boxes, painting them with broad brushstrokes. Humans are far more unique, their differences more nuanced, than any personality test can capture! At the same time, there is value in understanding some of the basic ways that people are different from one another. And that knowledge should have an impact on your leadership of them. Not knowing that someone needs time for processing, for example, while you are more impulsive in decision-making, will often cause the other person to feel like he or she was "run over" by you … not the best formula for communicating that you care about him or her.

Leaders can't know everything. But there are many things that you can and should know about those you lead, and in the end, this knowledge will enhance trust and the effectiveness of your leadership.

Gender

I'm sure you've noticed that men and women are different. Even with the push for equality between genders in the marketplace and other arenas, women and men are simply *not the same*—and the biology and science confirm it. Therefore, men leading women must always ask themselves, "What are the things that I am not even aware of because of my maleness?" Likewise, women leading men should ask, "What am I unaware of because of my femaleness?"

To think that men should think, feel, respond, and act like women, and vice versa, is to miss the real point of equality. Equality doesn't mean sameness *in every respect*. It does mean one gender is not superior to the other; both have value and both deserve respect. Men and women can be equal in rank, pay, and promotional opportunity while fundamentally different in how they operate in a professional setting, or in how they view and interact with the world. We don't need to perpetuate stereotypes that are unhelpful or outdated. But to not acknowledge gender differences not only leads to misunderstandings and hurts, but also causes you as a leader to miss out on the unique perspective and contribution that each gender offers.

This came home to me vividly after my first time coaching two of my daughters and their friends in basketball. I had grown up playing organized sports and had a variety of types of coaches. However, all of them had a similar trait in motivating us boys: they would get in our faces, yell at us, and challenge us to man-up to the challenge. Very few of the girls on my team had ever played basketball before our first game. We had one practice beforehand, when we worked on one play. Practicing that one play over and over, they seemed to have it down. However, as I soon found out, employing that play in the first game was another matter altogether. We were barely into the game when I quickly called a timeout. Drawing the girls into a huddle, I raised my voice a level or two, exhorting them to remember what we had practiced and to "get with it!" It was the same style of admonition I'd experienced from my own coaches years ago. *That should motivate them*, I thought to myself as they broke the huddle and went back on the floor. I think we lost that game 30–2.

As we left the gymnasium, my oldest daughter came alongside me, put her arm in mine, and said, "Dad, it really doesn't help when you yell at us." Her comment surprised me. And, yes, my initial thought, I confess, was that her remark revealed weakness or softness. But over time, I realized women and girls are simply different; both can work hard at basketball (or anything), but in general, they're not motivated in the same way as men and boys. And that's totally okay. As a leader and coach, I needed to remove my "male glasses" (my paradigm) and adjust my approach.

Race and Ethnicity

My wife and I have ten grandchildren. They are the joy and delight of our lives. Grandkids really are grand. Of our ten, nine are adopted and African American. This has been a wonderful experience for us, and it has also stretched us.

Race has never been much of an issue for me. I attended integrated schools from the early 1960s. My sports teams were integrated. Attending college, I became involved with an international mission agency with chapters in over 120 countries. I've seen many great changes toward a more equitable society since my early childhood in the 1950s, when I can remember the separate bathrooms and eating places. We have come a long way.

We also have a long way to go. And I have a lot to learn. I do not apologize for being a white, male American—it's who I am and who I will always be; I did not choose these facts about myself. However, as such, I have never been a person of color, a minority. Just as with the gender issue, I can't expect my understanding to be the same as someone of a different ethnic background than mine. To grow in this area, I've found that one of the better questions to ask a person from a different ethnicity is, "How do you see things from your position and experience?"

I was coaching some Southeast Asian leaders once and had visited them a number of times. Acquaintances were naturally developing into some friendships. There was a growing comfortableness among us.

Now, when I travel, I'm not out to promote my country. I am very grateful to be an American, but pushing America is not on my agenda. I truly enjoy the diversity of cultures and what each country adds to the global mosaic. One evening at dinner with this group of Asian friends, one person made a comment about government. I casually asked the group's perspective on the United States. He shared that most of the people in his country are afraid of America. My surprise was expressed in my response: "Why would you be afraid of us?" I asked him. He explained that they saw us as the world's most powerful country with the greatest military might on the globe, and though a current ally to his country, still the most powerful (human) force in existence. They, in contrast, were part of a small Asian country that one day might have the same experience as Vietnam.

Their perspective wasn't wrong just as mine wasn't right. We simply had different viewpoints. And because I was associated with the country they feared, to some degree, they viewed me with the same attitude. That conversation sparked a change in how I related to and helped those leaders. In particular, I worked harder at consciously seeking to know better who they were and the position they were coming from.

Generational Differences

When I was a senior in college, I remember a lively discussion in one class about generational differences. The professor was part of my parents' generation, and our class was giving him a rather hard time, suggesting how out of touch he was with us. I can still remember that we had a rather obnoxious smugness toward this "ancient" man. (My professor's rejoinder pulled us up short. He commented that the greatest generational gap was not between parents and their children but between seniors and freshmen. That put a stop to our remarks!)

As much as we thought we were the "in touch" generation, we weren't looking in the rearview mirror—nor were we aware of how fast the world was about to change before our eyes (soon making *us* the targets of the "out of touch" label).

In addition to getting to know your people as unique individuals, it's helpful to consider what is *generally true* of someone of their particular generation. For example, it might be important to remember that someone born in the 1990s or later can't recall a time when the internet and mobile phones didn't exist; they've grown up in a digital world.

Life Stages

Life is a journey with distinct stages. From new college graduates to parents of young children to empty-nesters and caregivers, life stage has a direct impact on levels of energy, availability, capacity, and interest. Leaders will do well to adjust their perspective and expectations in consideration of these stages.

One leader I'm coaching is a brand-new father. I asked him one morning how he and his wife were holding up with all the changes at home, including the middle-of-the-night feedings. His bleary eyes said it all. He asked me how long this phase lasted. I asked how many children they were planning on having. "At least two more," he replied. "Well, then," I told him, "you should plan on being tired for the next ten to twelve years." I'm not sure if that caused him and his wife to adjust their preferences or not. The point is that we have a mutual understanding of this new and drastically different life stage that he's entered—and the fact that he knows I know about his current situation helps him feel cared for.

Two of my colleagues, Paul Stanley and Dave Jewitt, have put together a Life Stages Chart that is handy for helping leaders realize their orientation in life's journey. In addition to aiding with understanding where you are right now, the chart lists critical questions asked at each stage, along with characteristics, dangers, and keys to succeeding in each stage. (This chart is provided in part III for your use.) Besides examining this chart, do some research if you need to; consider the life stages of those you lead, and ask others in similar situations what those stages or life circumstances were like. Get a sense of how you can better care for someone of a particular stage. For instance, a parent of a preschool-aged child may need to adjust her hours so she can drop off her kids in the morning before work. A parent of a special-needs child may have challenges you can't even imagine (and sometimes, the best strategy is simply to ask, point-blank, "What's it like to be in your situation?" instead of guessing).

Life situations don't excuse people from a failure to perform on the job they've been hired to do. But you can still be sensitive and caring—and aware that people's needs and concerns change as they enter different chapters of their lives. Staying up to date with their situations is important. You may get to know a person when he or she starts working for you at twenty-five years old, but that person isn't in the same place ten years later. The young professional who once stayed late hours at the office may now be married and need to go home to take care of a sick five-year-old.

Obstacles

There are obstacles to knowing people that may or may not be within your control as leader. These include a fear of being known and disinterest on your part.

The Fear of Being Known

On one level, everyone wants to be known. Someone showing an interest in us makes us feel valued. It's nice to be noticed and appreciated. On the other hand, we all, to some degree, can be afraid of being known, especially by people in authority over us. A 1999 book asked this question in its title: *Why Am I Afraid to Tell You Who I Am?* Author John Joseph Powell offers this answer inside: "I am afraid to tell you who I am, because, if I tell you who I am, you may not like who I am, and it's all that I have."[28]

Getting to know others and being known by others requires some risk on both sides. This reality can affect both you as a leader as well as those you lead. But the risk is worth it. Why? Because there's more to people than meets the eye. There's more to people, too, than what you might observe in a single context (such as at the office)—and they're influenced by factors well beyond that context. Every worker is more than a title or a name on an organizational chart; his or her contribution is greater than simply getting a job done (a robot can do that). If a

---

28 John Joseph Powell, *Why Am I Afraid to Tell You Who I Am?* (Grand Rapids, MI: Zondervan, 1999), 4.

person doesn't feel known or cared for by a leader, the personal tie will be lacking, as will his or her loyalty. He or she will be less likely to stay, care, do quality work, or go the extra mile.

I was coaching a young leader, Dane, on Capitol Hill who worked for one of his state's Senators. His office was directly across the hall from the Senator's, in fact. Dane put in long hours at relatively low pay and had being doing so for more than two years. Yet, when I first met him, he mentioned that he was job hunting. I asked him why. He initially shared all the benefits of being in the old Russell Senate Office Building on the Hill. The number and diversity of influential people who passed through the doors regularly was "a heady experience." To be exposed to so many national and international leaders was quite developmental, he admitted. However, he wanted to leave because his Senator acted as if she didn't even know who he was, despite the proximity of their offices and his tenure of service. Within a month, Dane had moved to a new position in the State Department.

In Dane's case, what level of "knowing" by the Senator would have been appropriate and appreciated? Here are a few facts he could've made an effort to find out: name, city where he was from, basic job responsibilities, and perhaps a few other personal details (e.g., birth year, favorite hobbies or interests, marital status, and/or areas of professional competence and expertise).

There is warrant for caution at this point. Knowledge can be misused. Some people can step over the line of appropriateness in how much they share—and social media has added a whole new variable to this equation. I had the privilege of working on Capitol Hill for a number of years. One of my responsibilities was to conduct an orientation for new Senate staff interns. One of the first principles I would drill into them was, "Information is never neutral on the Hill." To emphasize it, I would issue a slight variation of the Miranda Warning (shared by law enforcement officers when arresting an alleged criminal): "Up on the Hill, everything you say, everything you do, and everything you post CAN AND WILL BE USED AGAINST YOU!" I would expound on this, explaining, "People are watching you. They are listening to what you share and reading your posts on social media. Plus, it's easy to let this place get into your head, which can lead you to think that you have the authority to say things you shouldn't say and can get away with behavior that is inappropriate for this institution. And what is posted on social media has a very long life span. So be extremely careful."

Your own leadership environment probably does not have the same intensity and need for caution as Capitol Hill, but the principle is still true: information is never neutral. Moreover, if someone you lead has experienced hurt/betrayal by a leader in the past, he or she may be less apt to share personal information; so it's important to build trust and not become pushy or nosy. Additionally, some people will naturally be easier to get to know than others.

Disinterest

Besides the natural human fear of being known, another obstacle that may impede knowing your people is your own lack of interest. As a leader, you may wonder, "Why can't we just get on with the work and get things done?" Getting to know those you lead may feel both undesirable and unproductive.

And being task-oriented is fine … until it isn't. You will save yourself some time and grief by knowing more about your people at the outset. Otherwise, you will face the unenviable task of doing damage control after you make an offensive blunder that could have been avoided if you had taken the time and interest at the beginning to know your people.

Sarah valued a safe, friendly, predictable work environment. She excelled at her job as receptionist, and her quick smile put all who entered the door at ease. She was knowledgeable in directing inquirers to the proper office staff. At the same time, she was an effective gatekeeper, ensuring staff time was used well. She was just what the office needed at the front desk.

Sarah lasted less than a year. Max, the office manager, was a no-nonsense, get-the-job-done type of leader. He wasn't rude so much as he was distant. He knew what each staff member was hired to do, expected them to do that job, and that was about all he knew of each one. He couldn't understand why Sarah left. But any observer could've told you why: She felt very little care and personal tie to the office as a result of the coldness and disinterest of her immediate supervisor.

Know is the first Operational Aspect of Care, and it's also one of the hardest to implement. It is vitally important and yet fraught with obstacles and even dangers. Still, as a Trusted Leader, it requires action. The solution is not to refuse to get to know those you lead but to wade slowly and wisely into the waters of knowing your people without getting in too deep or too fast.

Chapter 13 Key Takeaways:

- To care well for those you lead, start with getting to know them; this shows you value them, not just for what they do but for who they are.
- What you should know about your people will depend on your leadership situation, but some considerations include differences in personality types, personal preferences, gender, race/ethnicity, generation (age), and life stage.
- Obstacles to this Operational Aspect include a fear of being known and disinterest in knowing those you lead.

Chapter 14
Care Operational Aspect #2: Connect

I was sitting in on a team meeting of an organization that had brought me in to coach their executives. One of the vice presidents, Dave, was explaining a decision that he and the CEO had made regarding an initiative that had been initially given to another of the vice presidents, Mary. This was the first time Mary had heard about the change.

As Dave continued to describe his new vision for this initiative, I could see Mary emotionally withdrawing. Tight-lipped and frequently looking down at her hands, she seemed to be fighting back tears as Dave droned on. Both he and the CEO had bypassed her, and they hadn't bothered to talk to her about it before this meeting.

Finally, as Dave wrapped up his explanation, Mary mustered the courage to speak. With trembling voice, she expressed shock and dismay at what she considered to be "backroom tactics" by Dave and the CEO. Her words revealed genuine hurt. Those around her looked alarmed—clearly unaware of how the shift in leadership of this initiative had taken place.

Unfortunately, Dave's response is one I've seen far too often in these types of situations. Immediately defensive, he retorted, "Mary, you don't understand. We had to take charge, and there are very good reasons we did it the way we did. You just have to trust us—this was the best course of action."

Mary wasn't satisfied. She wasn't going to give Dave an easy out in what she knew had been a very underhanded way of behaving. Yet, with every reply, Dave kept responding in the same manner: "Mary, you just don't understand."

The feeling in the room grew awkward at what became a two-way dialogue—a standoff, really. Finally, since I had a longstanding relationship with the team and I knew Dave and Mary both, I raised my hand and asked if I could share an observation. Everyone nodded.

First, I commended Mary for having the courage to speak up and "put it on the table." Next, I turned to Dave and asked if he grasped what he was doing in the interchange with Mary. Rather than acknowledging her hurt, he invalidated her feelings by only defending his actions. Here was one of his teammates who had been bypassed and then blindsided, and the only problem he could see was her lack of understanding. Needless to say, even if elements of what he was saying were right, he was missing an important opportunity to connect with her—and he was putting the unity of the team at risk in the process.

A Make-or-Break Aspect

Along with Know, Connect is the second of the two most difficult Operational Aspects of Care for most leaders. The tyranny of the urgent, demands of personnel, and pressures of production often pull you as a leader in a different direction. You also cannot meet every need or expectation. Plus, there are leaders who consider their responsibility to care for their employees completed when they hired them and agreed to pay them a salary.

However, for those leaders who understand that their greatest asset is those they lead, the effort to know and connect with their people pays huge dividends—resulting in organizational health and greater personal motivation among employees. Failure to know and connect with your people could result in the loss of top talent or the development (and persistence) of an unhealthy atmosphere.

What It Takes to Connect

So, how do you connect with those you lead? As a leader, you will need to offer your understanding, presence, time, attention, questions, and enablement.

Your Understanding

Connecting does not necessarily mean you agree with the other person. In the case of Dave and Mary, circumstances or contingencies may have necessitated that the initiative be assigned new leadership, and it's possible Mary would never have fully understood the reasons. But the point of connecting is not agreement—it doesn't mean you have to think the other person is right in his or her thinking and conclusions. The point is *understanding and recognizing how the other person thinks or feels*. It means acknowledging how another person is being impacted.

In Dave's case, rather than defend his decision, he could have looked Mary squarely in the face and said something like, "Mary, thanks for sharing that. I can see it hit you pretty hard, and I think if I were in your shoes, I would probably feel exactly the same way. I apologize for catching you off-guard with this." He could have then suggested taking a break in the discussion or offered to hear more of her thoughts on the topic after the meeting.

Beyond the corporate setting, think of a parent leading a child. Frequently, children don't know what's best for themselves—and they don't understand a parent's decision (nor do they need to!). But even as you remain firm in your decision ("No dessert until you finish your dinner"), you can still acknowledge the child's feelings, ("I understand you would much rather eat ice cream than broccoli, but the rule still stands").

Your Presence

A leader's presence says to those he leads, "You matter to me." Showing up makes a difference. This is sometimes known as "management by wandering around" and has been encouraged in the management literature for years. It is similar to the Japanese idea of the Gemba walk method, developed by Toyota. (*Gemba* means "the real place.") The idea is not to stay in your office or wait for people to come to you, but to "randomly" sample what is taking place under your supervision, at every level, simply by firsthand observation.

One can see the importance of the presence of someone we deem to be significant to us even in children. "Watch me, Mom," or "Watch me, Dad," are refrains echoed at the swimming pool as youngsters splash in the water or try going off the diving board for the first time. The presence of the parent is important to them.

And there are different levels of presence available to us today with varying degrees of effectiveness. A phone call is better than a text message or email. A video chat tops a phone call. But showing up in person says the most—like the parent who shows up for his daughter's basketball game.

When I was in student leadership work, my regional manager was Darrell Sanders. One of the things we looked forward to at least twice a year was Darrell's visit to us. He'd leave his wife and home in Memphis and spend three days with me and my family. Even our daughters enjoyed his times with us. In fact, when our oldest daughter was getting married, she asked Darrell to perform the ceremony.

On one of his visits with us, I introduced Darrell to a friend of mine, who later asked me what Darrell's job description was. I replied that, over the years of Darrell investing in me in these on-site visits, he had convinced me that his job description was to make sure that I made it. I shared that I knew his responsibilities were more extensive than that, but that was the essence of his job. My friend shook his head and said, "I'd give anything to have a regional manager with that job description." Darrell didn't simply write that he wanted a connection with me, and he didn't merely call from time to time (though he did both of those things, for sure). He demonstrated his desire to stay connected by coming and being with us. His presence spoke volumes.

Your Time

Related to being present, you also need to give your time if you're going to connect with someone. A three-day visit is not always an option in many scenarios of leadership. The next best thing is to give some of your time in some other way, whether through a note or phone call. In essence, you want to communicate to those you lead, "You're worth my time."

I have a wonderful family practice doctor. He's quite knowledgeable and personable. Whether it's a sore throat or the flu, he knows what to prescribe to take care of it. However, what I appreciate most about him is not his competence but the time he spends with me in the examining room. Upon entering, he sits down and immediately starts asking how I'm doing; it's as though he doesn't have anything else to do the rest of the day but listen to my concerns. Even with a waiting room full outside, his approach is that I'm the focus of his time. Whatever I need to ask him about, he has time for that.

I've had other doctors over the years who were nothing like my current doctor. Some always seemed to be in a competition for the number of patients they could see in one day. In and out in three minutes is the *modus operandi* for most general practitioners these days. They view their patients more as specimens and less as complete human beings. And we can develop the same distance or sense of impersonal disconnection in almost any leadership situation.

The most effective leaders are the ones who don't only get out of their office and "walk around" but who can also be "intercepted." That is, those they're around feel the freedom to stop them and engage them in some way. When the leader makes his/her time available to others in this way (at unplanned moments), while not doing so to an inappropriate extreme, a sense of connection is established.

Your Attention

Your presence and time are important. However, you take these connection points to an even greater level with your attention.

As a morning person, I'm often at my favorite coffee shop early in the day. With this routine, I get to observe certain recurring events. One that saddens me is that several father-son duos come in every morning, get their bagels, sit at a table, and proceed to pull out their smartphones. For the next twenty or so minutes, I watch as these two related males in extremely close proximity totally ignore each other.

I can still remember one of my young daughters trying to get my attention one evening as I read the newspaper. She kept repeating, "Daddy, can you look at my eyes? I'm trying to tell you something." By ignoring her request, I was communicating distance rather than a desire to connect with her (something I wish I could get a "do-over" on, now that I'm older).

As leaders, we can get so wrapped up in our own duties or importance that we begin to take for granted those around us. Giving others our attention doesn't take *all* of our time. It doesn't even take much effort. But it does take pausing a moment and concentrating on the other person.

When I once worked for a member of the U.S. Senate, I had my fair share of receptions—those "meet and greet" occasions that dot the calendars of every Senate office. It was interesting to watch how different senators handled these events. The responses weren't along party lines;

each political party displayed a wide spectrum of behavior. But one particular female senator offered such a contrast from another female senator that, frankly, it startled me.

This Senator's office had won a friendly wager with the other senator's office over a matchup in the NCAA basketball tournament. As payment, the other office furnished lunch for the sixty or seventy staff members of the other office. Notably, the winning office's senator showed up at the beginning and went around to every staffer shaking hands. For a little while (but no more than thirty seconds per person), that senator seemed able to give her full attention to each and every staffer. I thought, "Wow, I can see why she gets elected." The other senator (of the losing office), by contrast, came in for less than a minute, congratulated the winning office, and was gone. My thought toward her was, "I wonder how she ever got elected." (Now, I didn't know what the rest of her schedule entailed. Perhaps she had the President waiting in her office. However, it was remarkable that the other senator, as busy as all senators are, saw the importance of giving these staffers—of the opposing party, no less—a moment of her attention.)

Even though I had never met the senator of the winning office before, I couldn't help but feel some connection with her. There was a sense that "she stopped for me."

Your Questions

Another key way to connect with those you lead (or with anyone around you) is by asking good questions. Doing so takes the focus off yourself and gives others a platform and a voice. It allows them to be ones from whom you are seeking information and perspective. In essence, you're saying, "Help me understand. Help me to see what you see. I need your input."

As you walk around, you can observe what you see, but you can't *see* or understand the thinking of others. Asking questions helps you go beyond your own observations. When you listen actively to the answers, you are drawing others into your circle, which greatly enhances connecting.

I mentioned Darrell Sanders previously. He was great about calling up occasionally and saying something like, "Hey, Terry, I've been thinking about something and would like to get your thoughts on it. I'm wondering if you could help me think through it. Do you have a few moments to talk?" Then he'd proceed to tap my brain. As a young leader, I remember well thinking, "Wow, Darrell is asking for my input!" It wasn't a personal visit but almost as good.

I've found the following questions to be good starters:

- How are things going on the team?
- What are you most encouraged with?
- If you could see improvement in one area, what would that be?
- If we were to do this (project or whatever it is), what would you see are the pros and cons of that approach?
- Would you have a better suggestion? What would that be?
- Where are we stuck?
- What would be your thoughts as to a solution to this?

Your Enablement

As humans, we all seek approval of others. We may say we don't really need it, that we don't care what others think, but the fact is, we often do—especially from the leaders we admire. And giving that enablement is another way for us to connect with our team.

When our youngest daughter, Abby, got her driver's permit, we were living in the Washington, D.C., area. Traffic is no picnic. It's fast. Congested. Multiple lanes, especially on the Beltway. Needless to say, driving in D.C. is not for the faint of heart … and yet, it's a great place to enable someone.

Abby was so excited that she had passed the driving portion of the exam after earlier passing the written portion. She could now drive with a licensed driver in the front seat with her. As we walked to our car, I motioned for her to drive. She beamed at first, but only for a moment. As I directed her to head home on the Beltway (not via backstreets), her excitement turned to apprehension. "Are you sure?" she asked. I simply said, "Abby, you're a good driver. You've studied hard. You have a good bit of experience already. Since we live here, I want you to feel comfortable driving on the Beltway. I know you can do it. I have complete confidence in you." This wasn't flattery; every word was true. And she did really well. (By the way, her mom was not in the car with us, or the situation may have gone differently!) When we got home and Abby walked into our house, there was almost a glow about her. Part of that glow was a new connection with me. She was still my girl, but not my little girl. She was a young adult now with my full blessing.

As leaders, we can communicate care when we enable others to rise up and enter into who they are already becoming. As we recognize their progress, we show we care about them enough to spur them along in their development.

The Importance of Emotional Intelligence

As I have already mentioned, much has been written about emotional intelligence (EQ, as a parallel to IQ in the emotional realm). EQ is helpful for connecting well with your people. When we don't exercise good emotional intelligence, we offer numerous opportunities for disconnect. At its core, EQ is about being aware of (1) oneself, and (2) others, and using that dual awareness in a positive way. In other words, EQ is about both awareness and good management. Some questions to ask yourself include:

- Am I aware of what's going on inside me at this moment (e.g., that I'm getting angry, feeling threatened or attacked, feeling the need to defend myself, withdrawing)?
- Am I able to manage and control those feelings toward a positive outcome? Often, we are completely blind to what is happening within us even when it's obvious to everyone else.

Besides personal awareness, you need to be cognizant of your social environment:

- Am I aware of what's going on within other people? Am I sensitive to their verbal and nonverbal cues? Am I picking up on the subtle (or, in some cases, not-so-subtle) indicators that something big is happening inside those around me?
- Am I able to manage this social awareness toward a positive outcome? Am I able to harness the emotions of those around me, even negative ones, and manage them to achieve intended goals?
- How can I help them redirect their negative emotional energy toward positive solutions?

You may be asking, "Why is it such a big deal to be aware of how others are reacting?" Maybe you're not a touchy-feely type of person; you're not in touch with your own feelings much less those of others. "I do my job and expect others to do the same," you may think. "We can't stop every time someone gets their feelings hurt."

There's some truth to this—and I've seen teams become almost paralyzed with hypersensitivity to the possibility of offending someone. One of the executive teams I began to coach had relatively quiet meetings. My initial observation was that the managers were really nice and respectful toward one another. In reality, they were all holding their cards close to the vest in fear of provoking an offense. To help them with this, I put a small table in the middle of the room. I then looked for changes in facial expressions as the discussion progressed. When I saw one (an obvious reaction to a comment), I directed that person to "put it on the table." In response to their initial protests, I shared that the purpose of the meeting is to understand and move forward, not to avoid ideological conflict (to borrow Lencioni's term from *The Five Dysfunctions of a Team*). I explained that what they are feeling or thinking—often expressed by changes in facial expressions—may be the missing link(s) to finding the right way forward. By not putting their feelings and thoughts on the table, team members could be causing the whole team to miss a solution.

Remember my national presentation in which I had unwittingly shut down any pushback through a bulldozing attitude? What if I had been more in tune with how the audience was responding—noticing their body language, the dwindling number of questions asked, and other cues? I didn't do a good job connecting with the people listening. As a result, they didn't feel I would care about or listen to their objections, so they kept silent. This didn't benefit anybody!

Practical Steps

Connecting centers around communicating with others (e.g., with teammates, family members) that what's going on inside them is important to you. A practical step you can take to grow in this area is to use the Connect Tool in part III.

In addition, you can conduct an "audit" to connect with your group. The executive team I mentioned above did this very thing. The team members began by freely expressing what they were feeling and thinking without the fear of their words being used against them. They also began to spend time with each other in order to connect in different settings besides the executive team meetings. They began to conduct some of their sessions off-site, facilitating a more relaxed atmosphere. One person commented that she was beginning to see her fellow department heads as people and not simply as coworkers.

About two years later at this team's annual leadership meeting, I asked the chairman of the board what he was seeing as he observed these leaders. His comment was that he couldn't believe how many good leaders there now were in the organization and how much goodwill existed among them. We attributed this primarily to the fact they were learning how to demonstrate Care as they learned the practical steps of knowing and connecting with each other.

Chapter 14 Key Takeaways:

- Along with Know, Connect is a difficult but vital aspect of Care; without personal connection, employees are more likely to leave your firm, or others are likely to feel put off by your leadership.
- Connecting is not about agreeing with someone but about understanding and recognizing how another person thinks and feels.
- In addition to your understanding, giving your time, presence, attention, questions, and enablement will grow your connection with others.
- Emotional intelligence (EQ) helps you connect with others through a greater awareness of yourself and others, as well as understanding of how to act on that awareness.

Chapter 15
Care Operational Aspect #3: Provide

Jeff and Melissa lived in a suburban area of Colorado and were being considered for a more advanced leadership role in a student leadership organization that I oversaw. As the national director, I had the responsibility of visiting the couple and seeing whether they might be a good fit for this expanded role.

An energetic young couple, Jeff and Melissa had three charming children, all preschool-aged. I had met them a few times before, but this was my first time to be invited to their home for dinner. They had just recently moved into this new home and wanted to give me a quick tour.

As we sat down for dinner later, I casually asked Melissa, "Do you have a washer and dryer?"

"Oh, do you need something cleaned?" she responded quickly, surmising the reason for my question.

"Oh, no, but thank you for asking," I replied. "I was just thinking that with three small children, you must have a lot of clothes to wash frequently. I can remember when our girls were small. It seems like Sherry was doing a load or two of wash every day. I didn't notice machines anywhere in your house and just wondered how you do your laundry."

"I take them to a laundromat," Melissa replied a bit sheepishly, hurriedly adding, "We go on Mondays, Wednesdays, and Saturdays—it's just part of our weekly routine."

I looked between the two of them and said, "Well, let me ask you something. If I were to buy you all a washer and dryer set, would that be a help to you?"

"What do you mean?" Jeff asked, clearly wondering if there was a catch.

"Well, would it ease your workload to have a washer and dryer here in your home rather than taking the clothes to the laundry and having to watch the kids at the same time?" I asked. "I'd really like to pay for a set if it would be helpful."

Jeff looked stunned while Melissa started to cry. Both nodded.

"Super," I replied. "Why don't you shop around and find a set you like. Let me know how much it is, and I'll send you a check." And they did. And I did.

What and How Leaders Provide

As leaders, we can get so caught up with vision casting, inspiring, and organizing that we completely overlook one of the most obvious but critical Operational Aspects of Care: Provide. Providing means making sure that those we lead are supplied with the resources, materials, opportunities, and engagement they need to be successful in what they've been asked to do.

Tangible Provision

Leaders are often in the position of being able to provide material needs or funding that others cannot; we have the authority to allocate or reallocate resources to where they need to be. In the case of Jeff and Melissa, who were both involved in the work of an organization I led, I had the prerogative to offer assistance that would free up more of their time for the work they were hired to do. Notice, it took a physical visit to see this need. I quickly saw that loading up the kids two or three times a week and heading to a laundromat in town was an added and unnecessary strain—but I could also tell, just from observation of the way they lived, that their budget was tight, probably too tight to purchase a washer/dryer set anytime soon.

Providing will not always mean dipping into company (or even your own) pockets to meet a personal need like this—the resources you should provide will inevitably vary from situation to situation.

One way leaders can provide well for their people is by having a *leader's initiative fund*. I often share this concept with leaders of other leaders, especially in nonprofit scenarios or even with start-ups in the for-profit sector. This type of fund helps other leaders get "unstuck" in their job of providing. These funds allow leaders to move ahead, finish a project they started, or take care of a need that's holding them back or causing a strain on their team.

Nontangible Provision

Leaders don't only need to provide material things to those they lead but also intangible things, such as opportunities for their people to grow and engage with others, feedback, critique, encouragement, and even the permission to rest or take a break.

Many if not most people have an internal struggle focused on their own worth and abilities. Even leaders struggle with these feelings. As leaders, we need to show the people we lead that we believe in them. In other words, we need to provide positive reinforcement and encouragement.

One younger staff member, Matthew, on a team within my organization was not viewed very highly by some board members. I knew that their perception was based on very limited interaction with Matthew and, quite frankly, was unfair and skewed. Early in his employment with the agency, he had failed to adequately complete a couple of projects, though I knew from later evaluation that this was owing in part to some gaps in training new staff combined with other unfortunate circumstances at that time that had worked to his disadvantage. Nonetheless, the board members' minds had been made up early on, and I couldn't seem to change their view of Matthew.

Later, I was looking to introduce a new and improved training program for new staff. It was a program I had created at another agency, where I'd seen it work quite effectively. I knew it would help us. The only problem was, I was under the gun on multiple projects and my time was limited; I needed some help to pull together a compelling presentation to explain the program to board members before they met in less than a month. I immediately thought of Matthew.

From being with Matthew on a couple of trips, I could tell he was an underdeveloped leader who had been a bit stigmatized, even disillusioned, by the earlier critique of the board. I wanted to give him an opportunity to "reinvent himself" before the board, so I asked him to help me with this new staff training project. Initially skeptical, after a few weeks of working together, Matthew was really responding to my encouragement to take this project by the horns. He had even visited another organization where the program was in place; he was spending extra hours learning all he could about how the program could work well for us.

When Matthew began creating the visual presentation for the up-coming board meeting, his creative skills came to the fore. As he ran through the slides with me a few days before the board meeting, I knew it was top-notch. I couldn't wait to see the board members' reactions!

"We're ready! You're going to do great," I told Matthew. "They're going to love this—both the program and the way you present it."

Matthew jerked his head toward me as I spoke. With surprise in his voice he asked, "You mean I'm going to present this? I thought you were going to present it!"

I sensed his hesitancy; after all, he knew their perception of him. But I stuck with my decision and reasserted my desire for him to do the presentation. I told him I had all the confidence in the world in him.

Despite clear reluctance, he agreed, and he practiced the presentation several more times before the big day came.

On the day of the board meeting, I had Matthew wait outside the board room before he came in. I introduced the need for this project and then said that Matthew would be joining us and giving the presentation. The board chair leaned over to me and whispered, "I'd much rather you give the presentation, Terry." I thanked him for his confidence in me but reiterated my plan. Then I motioned for Matthew to join the meeting.

He gave a terrific presentation—so much so that, after he concluded, some of the board members asked him if they could sign up for the new training. I patted Matthew on the back and let him know he was released from the rest of the meeting. After he left, the board chair turned to me and asked, in front of the rest of the board, "How was Matthew able to do such a great job with that?" I responded, "If the raw talent is there, what all younger leaders need is to know that others they look up to care enough about them to provide them the opportunity to demonstrate that talent. To know that someone believes in them and will take a risk on them."[29]

In addition to providing opportunities for growth and development, we leaders also demonstrate care when we let those we lead get the *credit* they deserve. Too often, we use others to make us look good: they do all the work; we get all the credit. There's a quote, often attributed to either Ronald Reagan or Harry Truman (the original source isn't so important), that goes something like this: "It's amazing what you can get done when you don't mind who gets the credit." This spirit of humility can be hard (it goes against human nature), but it really does wonders for a team.

Unwelcomed Provisions

Most people will welcome the resources (tangible and intangible) that we as leaders provide them. But providing can take a not-so-enjoyable format (for those we lead) as well. I was chatting with the leader of a worldwide enterprise headquartered in Washington, D.C. Many years before our conversation, Thomas and I had both been affiliated with the same organization (a different one than either of us now worked with). I asked him what prompted him to leave that organization.

"Lorne fired me," he quipped, referring to the international president.

A bit surprised, I asked him, "Why did he fire you?"

"Insubordination," Thomas retorted. "Without a doubt, one of the best things that ever happened to me. Lorne could tell that I had a bent toward working with folks in the political arena. My constant swimming crosscurrent to where he was taking the work was causing a lot of undue friction on the team. He provided a giant gift to me by booting me off the team."

"A gift?!" I interjected, somewhat surprised by his label of his firing.

---

29 I recognize that in some situations, it would have been better for me to have given this presentation as the leader of the organization. But in this case, I made a strategic decision that I felt was appropriate and achieved two goals at the same time: making a presentation on an important new project *and* providing a critical chance for someone whom I believed could become one of our top leaders if we gave him the opportunity to "prove himself" (and prove the board's persistent view as dated and wrong).

"It humbled me, for one thing, and I needed that," Thomas continued. "It also freed me up to pursue my heart's passion. I wouldn't be here today, and this work would not be where it is, if Lorne hadn't provided me that lesson and that freedom. I am forever grateful to his discernment and courage to give me what I really needed."

Thomas's attitude toward being fired no doubt matured over the years; he came to recognize its value. This will not always be the case, and yet, sometimes the greatest way we can provide for those we lead is by giving them something they will perceive as negative (at least at the time). It may not be as drastic as a firing, but it may be just as unpleasant—a rebuke, a correction, a lecture, or the removal of some privilege, for example. Your job as a leader is to have the insight to know when these kinds of "unwelcomed provisions" are necessary and will ultimately be helpful to long-term growth.

One of my biggest concerns today for leaders of the future is what some call "snowplow" parents (also labeled lawnmower parents or helicopter parents). These are the ones who make sure that the roadway ahead is plowed so thoroughly that their kids are assured of never having to face any real obstacles or bumps along the way in their lives. They try to eliminate any unwelcomed provision.

While this impulse is understandable (who likes to see their children in pain, or floundering and failing?!), its consequences are extremely detrimental. Life is full of unwelcomed provisions. To become strong and healthy adults, young people don't need an absence of obstacles but, rather, the opportunity—and skills—to tackle obstacles head-on and to persevere and succeed through them.

As I write, one of the main headlines in the news today is about parents who allegedly bribed officials at top-level universities to get their children enrolled in those schools. These parents thought they were doing their kids a favor by helping them to succeed without trying. Imagine what their actions actually communicated to their kids! Essentially, they're saying that they didn't really believe their children had what it took to gain acceptance into the schools on their own merit. Rather than telling their kids they were going to have to get into the schools on their own (the unwelcomed provision), these parents gave them a welcomed provision that will bedevil them the rest of their lives—every time they look into a mirror knowing it was all based on a lie.

Joshua and Melinda had a different approach to the development of their kids. Whether it was sports, art, playing a musical instrument, or solving a complex math problem, the couple set goals intended to stretch their kids. When those goals were reached, a celebration occurred. "Way to go!" was easy to come out of their lips. Yet, there was no room for complacency. Along with the satisfaction of attainment was also the question of "How can you build on that? How can this achievement, as special as it is, be a new platform that can serve you for discoveries yet unseen?" It wasn't a message of being unsatisfied with their efforts and achievements; rather, it was the message, "I'm so proud of you. And I know there is still so much more of who you are that is yet to be revealed." In talking with their kids as adults, Joshua and Melinda said their kids never felt that they had to prove anything to anyone except themselves. "I wonder how far I can go in this?" became their own personal challenge to themselves every time they enjoyed another achievement.

Often what we consider achievement is mediocrity at best. It's like the sign on the wall coming out of the dressing room at the YMCA that says, "The only easy day was yesterday." We need the unwelcomed provision of personal challenge.

Avoiding Assumptions

For many of us leaders, we can think too broadly about provision for the needs of others. We see the big things: they showed up at the office today. They are clothed and somewhat in their right mind. They're not crying or angry. They have a budget to complete the project we gave them. "I guess they have everything they need," we can easily assume.

Our provision repertoire may be sorely limited.

A good exercise is to ask everyone you lead this question: "With what do you need to be provided in order to know that you are cared for?" The variety of answers you get may surprise you. Replies I've heard range widely; for example:

- Respect
- The "right tone" in others' voices
- The opportunity to be in on the process
- A vote on the decision
- The funding to get the job done
- Access to leadership
- Periodic review and assessment
- The opportunity to give input or make a contribution

The list can go on and on. Care is subjective and people's needs vary greatly. We each have our own set of "provisions" that we see as important, and we each perceive care in different ways.

In an earlier chapter, I mentioned Gary Chapman's book *The Five Love Languages*. Focused originally on the spouse relationship (how husbands and wives both give and perceive love), the principles are now applied more broadly to other relationships. The basic idea is that we tend to assume that everyone has the same "love language" we do. In the world of family and friends, these languages include gifts, quality time, physical touch, acts of service, and words of affirmation. If I feel most loved when my spouse gives me tangible gifts, but my spouse feels most loved when I spend quality time with her, then we may begin to feel *unloved* or uncared for if we don't understand our differences.

The same kind of disconnect can happen in the workplace when it comes to Care. I knew one leader who was infamous for never giving compliments. He would (rhetorically) ask, "Why should I give compliments? I don't need them. I do what I'm expected to do. I ask my employees to do what they are expected to do. Why give compliments for what's expected? If I don't need pats on the back, why should they?"

This leader didn't need to become a compliment factory, but he did need to work on understanding the very human need to be encouraged and positively reinforced in our work from time to time. His compliments didn't have to be doled out as frequently as others', but he did need to recognize that a total lack of compliments could be perceived as uncaring.

As leaders, we can't cater to every individual need or request, especially if we lead a large number of people; however, it's important to at least be aware of your own assumptions and biases in terms of what you think people need. As much as possible, seek a well-rounded approach to providing. In part III, you'll find a Provide Tool to help you evaluate how well you're providing for each of the people you lead right now in various areas.

Chapter 15 Key Takeaways:

- Caring involves providing others with what they need in order to succeed in what they've been asked to do, or in what they need to grow as a person.
- Provision may be tangible or intangible.
- We may provide what people think they need (welcomed provisions), and we may also provide what they don't think they need (unwelcomed provisions); both can lead to growth and success.
- It's important not to assume that you know exactly what people need in order to succeed. Use the tool in part III to aid with taking a well-rounded approach to providing.

Chapter 16
Care Operational Aspect #4: Protect

One of my coachees, Josh, was a regional director of an international NGO. He explained that he was preparing to appoint a replacement for the country leader in his field. Josh had asked a younger, inexperienced leader, Stephen, to take the role, mainly because he knew the nominee was eager to move up and usually had a hard time saying "no" to anything. Separately, I interviewed Stephen.

"Tell me about your experiences in accomplishing the goals of your agency," I began.

"Well, I haven't had a lot of experience with the actual fulfillment of those in my own territory," Stephen responded. "But I am deeply committed to the goals."

"How about some of the key progress indicators over the past six to twelve months? Where are you seeing some of the key areas of progress?" I asked him.

Again, Stephen was somewhat ambivalent on how he was doing, though he continued to reassure me of his belief in where the agency was going. As I continued to probe, it became clear to me that Stephen's enthusiasm far exceeded his actual work experience. He was charismatic. Articulate and winsome. I could see why Josh viewed him as a potential leader. Still, he was, in my estimation, about two to three years out from the level of responsibility for which Josh was tapping him. Future potential rather than demonstration of past results seemed to be the primary basis for the nomination. With the proper training, coaching, and proven demonstration, Stephen could possibly get there one day—but not now.

As Josh and I regrouped together, I shared my assessment, adding, "Given Stephen's lack of proper preparation and training, what are you setting him up for?"

Josh thought for a moment, dropped his head, and said, "I guess I'm really setting him up for failure."

"Exactly," I responded. "You will throw him into the ocean, and he will likely not make it. It will only hurt him and the organization in the long run."

I went on to explain the Operational Aspect of Protect. The regional director began to see that the opportunity he was trying to give an underdeveloped leader was ultimately premature and therefore an uncaring move on his part. Providing Stephen with a reasonable challenge was one matter; asking him to do with others what he had never done himself was quite another. Josh shifted to plotting how to retract the offer without insulting Stephen.

Clearing the Way

The fourth Operational Aspect of Care is Protect. This aspect entails defending, guarding, or shielding against attack, invasion, loss, injury, or danger.[30] While we can't and shouldn't protect those we lead from *all* harm, there are certain actions within our power as leaders that—with a measure of intentionality and discernment—we can take to prevent unnecessary or substantial harm from coming to those we lead. We can ensure that the risks or challenges that we allow and even encourage are reasonable ones, not foolish.

Protect is not about ascribing weakness to others and taking on the role of a superhero. It's about leveraging the authority you have for the good of those you lead—not to hand-hold or coddle them, but not to leave them exposed to harm that we easily could have prevented.

Let me illustrate. I was watching a special on television one day about ice-breaker ships. For some reason, I had the impression that these ships were used primarily to rescue other ships that had become encased in ice because they had ventured where they should not have gone at that time of year. This program, however, explained that most ice-breaker ships are used to keep shipping routes open. They move ahead of cargo ships, clearing the way for them to pass. Importantly, the ice-breaker ships are not towing the cargo ships, nor are they rescuing trapped ships. The ships that follow in the wake of the breakers are

---

30 Based on the definition in http://dictionary.com.

massive and free, moving forward under their own power and steerage. The breakers simply keep the channels open to ensure that the other ships can do what they were designed to do.

The Protect aspect of Care is similar. We should never enable our people in an unhealthy dependent relationship. We're here to "keep the channels open" for them.

Protect from What?

Leaders need to protect their people from themselves, certain failure, and other people.

Protection from Themselves

All of us are, at times, our own worst enemies. We have gifts and strengths, of course, but we also have weaknesses and blind spots, of which we may or may not be aware. Even if we're aware of our weaknesses, we may downplay them or decline to deal with them.

One day I was sitting in on an executive team meeting, where one of the leaders, Owen, was giving a presentation. I served as a coach to Owen, so I was watching him closely in his leadership role.

All of a sudden, one of the team members raised an objection. But instead of stopping and dealing with it, Owen essentially ignored the challenge and pressed on, much to the objector's frustration. After a few minutes of digging himself deeper and deeper into a hole, the rising tension in the room was unmistakable. Finally, I interrupted the dialogue and suggested it would be a good time for a coffee break. Pulling Owen aside, I suggested we take a quick walk together during the break. As we walked, I asked him, "What's going on inside you right now? What are you feeling?"

"I guess I'm a bit angry," he acknowledged.

"What do you think is triggering that anger? And I don't mean your colleague. What is your colleague's objection triggering in you that's driving your angry reaction?"

"I'm not sure," Owen said.

"Do you feel threatened by her questions? Are you sensing the need to protect yourself?" I asked.

He conceded that I was right and waited for me to go on.

"Your reaction is a very normal one," I told Owen. "When we feel threatened, our first reaction is to jump to self-protection. With you, your defensiveness takes on a tone of angry attack, though. Rather than letting the issue be the issue, *you* become the issue, and the result is your whole team shuts down. They don't feel like they can legitimately discuss the issue with you. Does that make sense?"

"I think you're right," he responded. "I can't erase what happened, so what can I do differently in this case?"

We chatted about some possible approaches to getting back on course, starting with an apology to the team. When we returned from break, Owen reengaged his team, apologized, and calmly addressed the objection that had been raised. The meeting moved forward productively.

My motivation as Owen's coach was not to take over the meeting or make him feel bad. My goal was to protect Owen from himself and help him grow in overcoming tendencies that were coming between him and his team.

When we protect those we lead, it's important not to purposely humiliate them in front of others; there may be a time and a place for a public rebuke, but most of the time, protecting people from themselves will entail quietly pulling them aside, one-on-one, and helping them see how their own faults are harming both themselves and others.

Protection from Certain Failure

You can probably think of an example of someone who was ready to step into a new responsibility but, for whatever reason, wasn't given the opportunity (perhaps a boss thwarted the rising leader's aspiration or simply didn't want to hand over the reins). This certainly happens. However, another scenario can play out, too, that is just as harmful to someone's future development and success: promoting someone to a higher leadership responsibility before he or she is ready and qualified, as illustrated in the anecdote with Josh and Stephen (at the beginning of this chapter).

Leaders can appear to be caring when—telling their people (with the best of intentions) that they "believe in" them—they tap people for higher roles. But if the people are not adequately prepared for those roles, then it's like throwing them toward a wall; when they hit the wall, the feeling of flattery quickly fades, and the new, in-over-their-heads leaders feel anything but cared for.

Leaders have the responsibility to protect those they lead not from challenges and opportunities for growth, and not even from *every* potential for failure, but from *certain failure.*

We set someone up for certain failure when we allow him or her to skip stages of development that are necessary to success.

Ken Blanchard's Situational Leadership model illustrates this well.[31] In his model, there are four development levels used to describe individuals. Everyone starts a new responsibility as an Enthusiastic Beginner. Eagerness far surpasses competence at this point, but it's just where she is. We see her potential, though, so we promote her. In her new role, her competence is still fairly low. She has entered what Blanchard labels the Disillusioned Learner stage. She begins to question her own abilities and suitability for the role: she encounters situations she hasn't experienced before, people don't respond the way she expects, and discouragement starts to settle in. This is the stage where most leaders are lost and don't progress; most leaders don't want to deal with the failure or sense of inadequacy, so they step out.

If she hangs on, though, she will continue to grow in competence and commitment, and she'll become what Blanchard calls a Reluctant Contributor. Eventually, people in this stage progress to Peak Performers.

Now, imagine what would happen if we promoted our aspiring leader too early, or to a position for which she wasn't ready? We think this shows how much we value her and her abilities and contribution. It's the "let's throw her into the middle of the pond to see if she can swim" approach to development. But instead of setting her up for wild success, we're actually setting her up to fail and to become *so* disillusioned that she's very likely to drop out and not even keep trying.

---

31 Ken Blanchard and Paul Hersey, *Situational Leadership, Online Leadership Training for High-Performing Leaders,* https://www.makeadentleadership.com.

Now, every Enthusiastic Beginner, to some extent, gets in over his head. That's part of learning. However, it's one thing to be in over your head in the shallow end of the pool; it's another thing to be in over your head in the deep end before you've learned to tread water.

Every Enthusiastic Beginner, according to Blanchard, will hit the Disillusioned Learner stage at some point. But how he got there (and how deep in disillusionment he is) is important, as is your role in walking the person through this stage in a caring, development-mindset manner.

I know one executive director whose classic line to those on his team who were struggling (i.e., the Disillusioned Learners) went something like this: "Why can't you do it? Rob is doing it. Susan is doing it. Why can't you do it?" Rather than protecting his people from their own inner doubts and fears, he exacerbated them. Rather than protecting *them*, he was protecting *himself* by essentially saying, "It's not my fault you're struggling. It must be a problem with you." Needless to say, that director had a long string of disgruntled former employees!

Parents can easily do the same thing. I've seen this primarily in the disengaged parent who, through either choice or necessity, places her children in the position of being a "latchkey child." These kids may be able to find a way to fend for themselves, but they are still children. And children have the wisdom of children. Failure in some way—perspective, thinking, behavior, or reactions—is bound to happen. (It's not a question of if failure will come but when.) Too much freedom and independence does not protect the very young from certain failures.

Protection From Others

To varying degrees, we all deal with challenging people and hostile environments. Office politics, interpersonal conflicts, misbehavior, and anxiety and self-doubt can plague us. As a leader, we cannot protect those we lead from every potential personal conflict (even if we wanted to!). But we can and should strive to set a healthy tone, a mutually encouraging and collaborative atmosphere.

When our people are being hampered from productivity and success due to a pattern of bad behavior in some (or one person) on our team, we have the responsibility to use our authority to step in and do something about it. I had a personal experience with this that I'll never forget.

I had been asked to give a four-part lecture series to the leaders of one of the major departments in my company. I was part of a different department, and these two departments didn't always appreciate each other. To say I began the series with some nervousness was an understatement. I was confident in what I had to share, but I was nervous as to how the leaders would respond.

After my first lecture, a number of the leaders came up and commented on how much they appreciated the talk. They looked forward to the rest of the series. They proceeded to ask some questions about the first talk and seemed genuinely interested in my answers.

All was going well until I got to the last three leaders in the line. Instead of asking a question, one of them made an opening statement on behalf of the remaining trio, saying they knew all of this already, and they didn't need me to come in and tell them what they already knew. It was brutal, especially because I was much younger than them.

Feeling like I'd been run over by an eighteen-wheeler, my natural instinct was to cancel the other three lectures. I was sitting on a bench, contemplating how I could get out of the rest of the talks, when I saw my department head, Paul, almost running to where these three leaders were huddled. He confronted them. Finally, they sheepishly strolled over and apologized for their behavior. Then Paul came over and reassured me of my lecture and the absolute necessity of the other three talks. I've never forgotten the difference Paul's protection of me made in the rest of that series.

Avoiding the Extremes of Under- and Over-Protection

The concept of Protect may evoke a significant aversion in you. In some cultures (especially America's), individualism and self-sufficiency are such strong values that no one wants to appear to be needy—or to be enabling neediness in others. In this age of all sorts of sensitivities— whether it's gender, ethnicity, age, or some other characteristic—the sentiment that "I can take care of myself, thank you" is a prevalent and powerful one. Thus, those you lead may resist the very idea of your protecting them.

Some reasons for people's repulsion to protection are valid. For example, many leaders, admittedly, have failed hugely in this area, especially with respect to women and children. It's no wonder we don't trust or even desire our leaders to protect us anymore—they have failed us in the past so many times by abusing their power for their own pleasures, purposes, and advancement rather than using their authority for others' good. Violations of contracts, agreements, and promises are rampant. Massive layoffs have occurred and whole businesses shut down because leaders' personal ambitions and failings got the best of them. So, let's face it: it makes sense why so many people may reject the idea of being protected by those they don't trust because of past harm.

On the other end of the spectrum, some leaders take such a delight in protecting their people that they assume a patronizing stance and end up being overprotective. Their actions and words communicate the message, "It's a good thing I'm here because you need me here to protect you. I'm smarter than you. I'm stronger than you. I'm more experienced than you. Where would you be without me? Just sit quietly. Take notes. I've got you covered."

By including Protect under the umbrella of Care, we do not want to perpetuate these extremes. Leaders should avoid both under-protection and over-protection. Just because abuses exist does not mean this aspect isn't important or beneficial when done correctly.

Morris was one of our up-and-coming leaders. I had pulled him onto our launch team to give him experience at a national level. This team was to serve for two years to prepare for a major shift in our organizational structure. Morris's contribution was most helpful. However, at the end of the two-year launch, I did not ask Morris to be on the new national leadership team. Instead, I asked him to focus on his region, assuring him that his time would come for greater leadership. Despite my assurance, I could tell he was hurt.

Six years later, Morris was asked to become our national director. As we talked about all that had transpired, I asked him his perspective toward not being asked six years earlier to be on my executive team. He indicated the memory still stung slightly. I asked his permission to share my perspective (which he granted).

"I knew you were going to be one of our key future leaders," I said. "However, I also knew that dissolving nineteen regions over those next two years in order to create one national operation was going to involve a lot of organizational politics, labeling, and cliques—something that would not serve you long term. I wanted you to miss most of that so that when the dust settled, you would not be labeled with a particular faction. Instead, you would be seen as being 'above the fray' and one of the leaders agreeable to everyone. And that's exactly what happened." He smiled and nodded.

Part III offers a tool you can use to evaluate how you can and should be protecting those you lead. You as a leader are in a unique position to leverage your role, authority, and power to afford a level of protection that only you can provide. I often think of it as being in a foreign city like Paris and trying to navigate the streets and subways for the first time. It's easy to get lost. One can find one's way around with enough work and resources such as a smartphone with GPS. However, a Parisian has personal authority and knowledge that no electronic device (not to mention a foreigner) can afford. That special knowledge adds a higher dimension of protection. And those who avail themselves of (and heed) the protection of their leaders are wise.

Chapter 16 Key Takeaways:

- Leaders protect those they lead in order to prevent unnecessary harm from befalling them; it is not hand-holding or coddling but a "clearing of the obstacles" in a waterway.
- Protection isn't a sign of weakness of those under a leader; rather, it signals the unique position a leader is in, as a result of his or her authority and/or special access to resources and knowledge.
- Leaders have a responsibility to protect their people from three main threats: themselves, certain failure, and others.
- Some people are repulsed by the concept of protection due to experiences of past abuse (leading to extreme tendencies toward under- or over-protection); these concerns are valid, but when done correctly, protection can be hugely beneficial.

The LDC model integrates interrelated actions, which should be combined and carried out with intentionality, undergirded by a shepherd's heart for the people you lead.

Care: Operational Aspect Summary

Leading people well entails caring for their well-being. People aren't just means to your end—they are human beings, not human doings, and should be valued for their own sake. Caring for those you lead means responding to their needs in appropriate ways. It helps avoid wrong assumptions and misunderstandings that can lead to unnecessary conflict and dysfunction. The four aspects of Care—**Know, Connect, Provide,** and **Protect**—are interwoven. Without Knowing and Connecting with people, for example, you cannot properly Provide for or Protect them.

In Action

Kirk expressed a desire to lead his teenage son, Parker, better. More specifically, Kirk expressed to his own mentor, Heath, that he felt he needed to provide his son with more opportunities to be engaged in team sports. Why did he feel that? Heath asked him. Kirk then shared how he had been very engaged in team sports himself as a teen, and how much he had grown as a person through the competition and challenges that team sports afford. Out of care for Parker, Kirk didn't want to be remiss in not providing his son with similar opportunities for growth. Before agreeing, Heath pressed Kirk further—asking what activities Parker really enjoyed doing in his spare time. "I'm not sure," Kirk replied—suddenly aware that he had been projecting his own preferences on his son without realizing it. Heath challenged Kirk to spend some time with his son and find out what he really liked to do if he could set his own agenda. When he did this, Kirk was surprised to learn that his son didn't like team sports at all. His real interest was in art. This discovery helped Kirk see that his attempt to Provide for his son had not been based on Knowing his son.

Chapter 17
Using the Model

Our overview of the Lead, Develop, and
Care (LDC) Leadership Model is now
complete. Having covered it piece by piece,
I could leave the impression that it is,
basically, a bag of tools. As I've said from
the beginning, however, this is an integrated
model. It is most useful and powerful when
applied in whole rather than in part. Like
musicians in a symphony or basketball players on a court, this framework yields results
greater than the sum of its individual parts.

Nonsequential, Overlapping Responsibilities

Before moving on to some practical steps to using the model, two caveats
are in order.

First, although we always explain the components of the LDC model in
the same order (Lead first, followed by Develop, and lastly Care), you
need not begin applying its components in that same order. In fact, you
should tailor the order of implementation to your unique leadership situation. For example, when forming a new team, it's usually best to focus
on the Operational Aspects of Lead first. Since you recruited the team
members, and they've opted in, they likely already have some degree
of trust in you. Their first questions will relate to what they need to do.
But what if you inherit an existing team? In that case, it's often better to
start with an emphasis on Care—specifically, the Operational Aspects of
Know and Connect. This allows you to build the trust and safety that you
need to focus on Lead. Once Care and Lead are carried out adequately,
you will have enough connection and momentum to engage the team
members developmentally.

Some have compared the model to a rotating "fidget spinner." One prong isn't more important than the other—all are needed—but the one with which you start won't be the same for every team or leader. Instead, you should determine which of the Primary Responsibilities is most needed right now. Once you answer that question, start applying the model in that area and then rotate through the other two based on what is most appropriate for your situation. Eventually, all three of Lead, Develop, and Care should be in practice, working in tandem.

A second caveat relates to the overlapping nature of the Primary Responsibilities. Carrying out one Operational Aspect may necessitate carrying out another one (or two) concurrently. For example, a person you're leading might be most in need of development, but you will have to employ certain aspects of Lead to help her Develop—which in turn will mean you are providing for and/or protecting her in some way (Care). Despite this overlap, your central focus (with this particular team member, for the time being) is Develop.

Getting to Work

Let's look at some ways to use the LDC model in your own leadership situation(s).

Using the Model in Planning

Intentionality in leadership means not waiting for there to be a "fire" to put out. An intentional leader thinks ahead proactively as a matter of course. Here are two practical ideas, one at the macro level and another at the micro level, for helping you with regular, ongoing application of the LDC model. (Adapt these ideas as desired to fit your own situation and rhythm.)

Idea 1—Macro-Level Planning (see Intentionality and the Primary Responsibilities tool in part III): Set aside some time every month (e.g., 90 minutes on the first Monday of each month) to think at a high level about how you are doing in using the LDC model with all those you lead. What or who needs attention? What step(s) should you take to address this need? Pick a time and frequency for this planning period that is right for you and try it out for a few months. You can always adjust it if you need to.

Idea 2—Micro-Level Planning (see LDC Planning tool in part III):
Take a set amount of time per week (even if it's only 10–15 minutes) to think about each of your direct reports in light of the Operational Aspects. This time will refresh your mind about your intentionality with each person and team. The sample form provided in the tool shows one way to collect your thoughts during this planning time. You don't need to fill in every box every week. If you have six direct reports, you could plan on an hour each week to give 10 minutes of thought to each person. This may not seem like a lot of time, but it's likely longer than you are currently spending, and it's a good place to start.

Using the Model in Diagnosing

Problems of varying kinds—specific conflicts, misunderstandings, poor performance issues, failures in alignment, and on and on—inevitably arise when leading people and teams. The acrostic **F.A.C.E.** can help you gain a clearer understanding of these issues and your role as a leader in addressing them.

Focus—What is the leadership opportunity or challenge at hand? Briefly describe it in a sentence or two. What is the main issue?

Ask—Which Primary Responsibility is most needed right now to address the situation? Is this primarily a Lead, Develop, or Care issue (or a combination of two)?

Clarify—Within the Primary Responsibility you just identified, which Operational Aspect(s) is most needed now? For example, if you are dealing with a Lead issue, what is most needed: Set Direction, Align, Motivate, or Manage? If the issue falls under Care, is there a deficiency in Know, Connect, Provide, or Protect (or a combination of two or more of these things)?

Engage—What are the next steps? What will help you take action? Which steps would make the biggest difference the soonest?

This acrostic is a suggestion to get you started with diagnosing problems (see the FACE Tool toward the end of part III).

Each person's situation, context, and personality are unique. Use these ideas as a springboard, knowing you will be happiest and most successful with a format that you have had a hand in creating and adapting.

Conclusion

Congratulations. You've read the whole book. This means you are interested in being a great leader who leads, develops, and cares for those who look to you for leadership. That's my hope for you as well.

After teaching and coaching this model for the past twenty years, it has become clear to me that the greatest gifts of the LDC model can be summed up in three words: clarity, practicality, and intentionality.

Clarity is a huge gift. One of our key goals has always been to help "take the mystery out of leadership." We often hear people at the end of our seminars say, "I've got it. Leadership finally makes sense to me!"

Practicality means it can be done. Along with "I've got it," we frequently hear, "And I can use it next week." A leadership model has to work. I trust that the many tools and exercises included in this book prove (or will soon prove!) its practicality.

Intentionality means you are not just trying to get a job done (whether it's making a profit or scoring more touchdowns); you are leading people. LDC assists you and prods you to communicate in tangible ways with those you lead to let them know they are visible and valued. The model truly helps you become a trusted leader, a leader others want to follow.

If the greatest gifts of LDC are clarity, practicality, and intentionality, the biggest barrier to these benefits is the model's sustainability. LDC can't be just one more thing you do, or it will only be a matter of time before you stop doing it. To really work, LDC needs to become the way you do everything when leading others. It must be woven into every aspect of planning, executing, and evaluating so that, eventually, it becomes instinctual—an invisible scaffolding, always there in the background, providing the natural and inescapable frame of reference for how you lead.

After presenting the LDC concept all over the world, my colleagues and I have made a key observation: Getting coached in your leadership using this model will make an even bigger long-term difference than simply reading this book or learning the model on your own. Talking through your leadership situation with someone else, with the LDC framework as a guide, helps you build the habits of thinking that ensure its ongoing application and benefit. LDN Global has a roster of certified coaches who would be happy to engage with you if this interests you. You can find out more at leaddevelopcare.com.

In closing, you face two challenges: (1) initially learn and apply the model; and (2) look at all the ways you can sustain its use in your life for the rest of your leadership career. And remember, this model isn't just for the workplace. It's also imminently valuable in your home and family, self-leadership, group sports, faith community, and many other settings.

Already, you are well on your way to becoming a different kind of leader: a leader who naturally, constantly, and wisely leads, develops, and cares. Our LDNGlobal team is here to cheer you on. Let us know how we can help.

Part III
Tools & Exercises

Lead Tools

Develop Tools

Care Tools

Using the Model

Set Direction Tool

(Six Questions)

1) Think through a situation for which you need to set direction. For the questions in the first column below, use the middle column to write your initial thoughts on the answers. Refer to chapter 5 for more guidance.
2) Next, discuss your initial responses with someone. Ask the person if he/she sees any gaps or blind spots in your thinking. Ask if your responses are clear and concise. Based on this discussion, add any further thoughts in the third column.

	Initial Thoughts	Further Thoughts
Who should be involved in setting direction?		
Where are we going?		
Why are we going there?		
What does success look like?		
What are our current realities?		
Which boundaries are needed to meet our target?		

ACTION POINT: Write out one tangible step you will take and when you will accomplish it.

Align Tool #1

(Alignment of Thinking: An Audit of Group Attitude)

1) Review the Set Direction Tool and determine who is involved.
2) Respond to the following questions in column one, and write your initial thoughts in the middle column.
3) Once you are finished, discuss your initial responses with someone. Ask if he/she sees any gaps or blind spots in your thinking. Discuss additional ways you could address the alliances in your context. Based on your discussion, add any further thoughts in the third column.

	Initial Responses	Further Thoughts
Is everyone "all in"? Why or why not?		
How are alliances (factions, cliques, circles of friends) having an impact on the group as a whole?		
What are the alliances about?		
How might the issues the alliances are causing be addressed?		

ACTION POINT: Write out one tangible step you will take and when you will accomplish it.

Align Tool #2

(Alignment of Actions)

This tool is used for aligning goals of an individual, couple, family, group, team, or project.

1) Review the six questions in the Set Direction Tool before proceeding.
2) Desired Result: Determine the first goal you want to achieve and write it down in the box at the top of the chart on the following page.
3) Right Things: In the first column, write down the top four actions that must be accomplished for your goal to be achieved.
4) Right Way: In the middle column, write down any qualifiers or descriptions of the actions from column one. Ask yourself, "What is the best way(s) to do this action?"
5) Right Time: As you look at what you have written, look for actions that are interrelated or sequential. Ask yourself if there are some that must be in process or finished before another can start. Are there actions that need attention daily, weekly, or at some other regular interval? Use the right column to sequence the four actions (numbering them 1 through 4).
6) Replicate the chart and repeat this process for the other goals that must be accomplished to achieve your desired end result—breaking up each one into manageable and sequenced actions.

Desired Result:		
Right Things	**Right Way**	**Right Time**

ACTION POINT: In the far right column above, under or beside your sequencing numbers, write the date(s) when you will start and complete each action.

Align Tool #3

(Alignment of Resources)

1) Review your answers to the six questions in the Set Direction Tool before proceeding.
2) Fill in the chart below, following the instructions in the left-hand column for a task at hand—perhaps one of the actions from Align Tool #2.

Brainstorm a list of resources (things and people) needed to accomplish the task. When you are finished, **underline** what you **have** and **circle** what you **need**.	<u>Things:</u>		<u>People:</u>		
Prioritize the importance of your circled needs.	1.	2.	3.	4.	5.
What are possible ways to secure what you need?					

ACTION POINT: Write down one step you are determined to accomplish after doing this exercise.

Align Tool #4

(Alignment of People)

1) Review your answers to the six questions in the Set Direction Tool.
2) Fill in the chart, following the instructions below with regard to a current project or goal.

For a New Project		For a Current Project
Consider the **roles** that need to be aligned. (What "seats on the bus" are needed?)		Consider the **people** that need to be aligned. (Who is currently in which "seats on the bus"?)
Fill in the "Thoughts to Convey" column of this form with one role in mind.		Fill in the "Thoughts to Convey" column of this form with one person in mind.
Next, set an appointment with prospective candidates and fill in the "Reactions" column during the meeting.	OR	Next, set an appointment with that person and fill in the "Reactions" column during the meeting.
Finally, fill in the last column and schedule additional appointments to work through any alignment issues.		Finally, fill in the last column and schedule additional appointments to work through any alignment issues.

	Thoughts to Convey	Reactions on Alignment	Further Steps
Project:			
Prepared for (Name):		**Meeting Date and Time:**	
Where are we going?			
Why are we are going there?			
What is the contribution needed from this role?			
Describe the person you need for this role. **OR** Why is this person currently in the role?			
What does the role look like when done well?			
Why is it critical to the overall project that this role be done well?			

ACTION POINT: Write down one step you are determined to accomplish after doing this exercise.

Align Tool #5

(Leader Selection Chart)

1) Review the chart below.[32]
2) Answer the Action Point questions.

Organizational Considerations *What exactly is the role,* *and what does the ideal* *candidate look like?*	**Individual Considerations** *Is the candidate willing to do* *the work, and is he/she* *suited to leadership?*
CONTEXT • Written job description • Industry knowledge • Time frame • Goals & expectations • Existing structures 1	3 • Desire • Energy • Openness • Courage • Resilience **WILLINGNESS**
FIT • Critical success factors • Cultural values • Relevant experience • Temperament & personal qualities • Necessary skills 2	4 • EQ & IQ • Deportment • Organization • Learning channel • Adaptability • Communication **CAPACITY**

ACTION POINT: Answer the questions on the following page pertaining to each quadrant above.

---

32 © 2019 Jess MacCallum. Used by permission.

Organizational Considerations

CONTEXT— *What exactly are you looking for?*

- Written job description: What are you asking the person to do? Be as precise as possible.
- Industry knowledge: What kinds of knowledge will be essential to success? What does the candidate need to understand about the audience you are serving?
- Time frame: When must a decision be made? If there is a deadline to find someone, it will influence the selection process; you may need to revise expectations based on available candidates.
- Goals and expectations: How will the person know if he or she has succeeded? How will you know? Success can be measured in both results and habits. Clarity will avoid conflict.
- Existing structures: How does the role fit into the whole organization? You need to understand how the new role will fit into the larger picture, because questions will arise.

FIT— *What does the ideal candidate look like?*

- Critical success factors: What habits are needed to succeed as a leader in this role? Will the person be writing reports, dealing with groups, counseling one-on-one, in charge of his or her own schedule?
- Cultural values: What values does the organization want its leaders to embody? Is the work fast-paced, relational, service-oriented, needs-based?
- Relevant experience: What past experiences are necessary to this role? Sometimes a candidate must have certain personal experiences to understand the role.
- Temperament and personal qualities: Is there a personality component to success in this role? Does the role need a charismatic personality, a quiet listener, a networker?
- Necessary skills: What specifically does the role require that is nonnegotiable? (Is writing or public speaking essential, for example?)

Individual Considerations

WILLINGNESS— *Is the candidate willing to do the work of leading?*

- Desire: Does he or she want the challenges of leadership? Not all who seek leadership roles truly understand what comes with it.
- Energy: Is the person willing to put in the time and energy required to lead well? Leading is different than doing the work itself, but often a leader does both. Energy is essential.

- Openness: Is he or she willing to learn from the team, the boss, and peers? Is the person teachable and willing to change behavior when given good reason?
- Courage: Is the person willing to face tough times and tough people? Times of testing are part of the deal.
- Resilience: Is the person willing to give it his or her best effort every day? Will he or she put yesterday in perspective and face today as a new opportunity?

CAPACITY— *Is the candidate actually suited to leadership?*

- Emotional intelligence: Is this the right time for the person to take on this role, or does he or she need more seasoning?
- Deportment: Does the candidate present himself or herself well to every audience with whom he or she will interact? Does the person carry him- or herself in a way that brings credibility to the work, or does he or she present an unnecessary obstacle? (Example: Does the person have reasonable manners, dress appropriately for the situation, grasp the social cues around them, etc.?)
- Organization: Is there a real capacity to balance tasks, time, people, budgets, materials, goals, and reports? Demands present challenges, and a leader must be able to balance them without excuses.
- Learning channel: Is the person a learner, aware of how he or she learns best? Does the candidate demonstrate a history of intellectual, emotional, and professional growth? Does he or she know how to "feed" him- or herself in this regard?
- Adaptability: Can the person navigate changing situations and maintain balance? In an ever-changing world, how well can he or she deal with interruptions, complaints, crises, and human weakness, and still keep the team on task?
- Communication: Does the person understand the value of clarity, and can he or she achieve it? Is the person a proactive communicator who can develop people and build teams using clear and honest communication?

Motivate Tool

1) Across the top of the chart on the following page, write the names of those who look to you for some level of leadership.
2) Make your best educated guess at what motivates or energizes these three people; put a check in the corresponding box(es) along with your reasoning.
3) Now, validate your assumptions through observation and conversation, and then fill in the boxes in the corresponding rows of the chart. We suggest that you ask the people directly what they feel are their two top motivators.
4) In the final row of the chart, write down specific ways that you could energize each person by tapping into their motivations.

	Name 1:	Name 2:	Name 3:
Rewards			
Consequences			
Security			
Appreciation			
Empowerment			
Development			
Purpose			
Competition			
Validate and apply your assumptions and then fill in the next two rows.			
Observation			
Conversation			
ct on what you've discovered.			
y(s) to rgize this n according her tor(s)			

INT: How can you develop the habit of knowing and utilizing your nary motivations?

Manage Tool #1

1) Self-evaluation: Rate your perception of your current effectiveness in four areas of the Operational Aspect of Manage. Use numbers 1–5 (filling them in in the "Score" column), where 1 = never true of myself, 2 = rarely true of myself, 3 = at times true of myself, 4 = usually true of myself, and 5 = always true of myself.
2) In the column on the far right, considering your scores, explain how your management skills in planning, organizing, guiding, and assessing have an impact on your overall leadership.
3) If possible, have a conversation with someone to verify your self-evaluation and thoughts concerning your managing abilities. It may be valuable for you to seek the input of others through a 360-degree review or a coach.

Planning		
	Score	How is this having an impact on your leadership?
I have a good understanding of our goals, and I can clearly articulate them to others.		
I perceive what steps are needed to get from the present situation to a desired goal.		
I review my active plans weekly to mark progress and make adjustments.		
Those involved in a project with me know where we started, where we are, and where we are headed.		
I am comfortable adjusting my plans according to unforeseen circumstances that arise.		
I watch for issues that will disrupt plans and work to solve them before they block progress.		
Planning Score		out of 30 possible

Organizing		
When I divide work among people, I try to ensure that no one is bored or overworked.		
My direct reports clearly know what their roles are and are familiar with the roles of the others on the team.		
My calendar shows that I have organized my time, giving priority to the strategic needs of each day.		
I regularly have team meetings with an agenda that I have prepared ahead of time.		
My schedule and calendar are organized so that I know today's agenda and am confident to re-schedule in the moment if needed.		
I respond to correspondence in a manner that does not require those important to me to remind me or resend.		
Organizing Score		out of 30 possible
Guiding		
I clearly understand the job description (role) of each of my direct reports and how I expect that role to be executed.		
My direct reports clearly understand their job descriptions and how I expect them to be executed.		
I have a plan to spend time with and observe my direct reports, and I follow my plan.		
I know the personality type of each of my direct reports so that when I give feedback, it is personalized with the greatest chance of being well received.		
I am approachable and available to those who need to contact me for important issues.		

I spend enough time with my direct reports to allow me to evenly compliment and correct them.		
Guiding Score		out of 30 possible
Assessing		
I understand and appropriately use an assessment system (e.g., job descriptions, periodic reports, performance reviews).		
When I sense when my direct reports are bored, frustrated, or overworked, I speak as transparently as I can with them about expectations and adjust as I am able.		
My direct reports and I meet for regular performance checks in addition to required performance reviews.		
When I hear that one of my people may have conflicting thoughts with our plans, I first take time to observe and listen directly to them.		
I see progress made with the recommendations that I make to my direct reports during our interactions.		
I would not remove or transfer a direct report without first implementing a plan with him or her to develop the person to the expected level.		
Assessing Score		out of 30 possible

ACTION POINT: Write down one step you are determined to accomplish after doing this exercise.

Manage Tool #2

(Leverage and Develop Management Planning Tool)

1) Consider how you can leverage each management skill (planning, organizing, guiding, and assessing) in your current and future leadership. From the previous tool, pick a self-assessment statement from each skill area in which you scored yourself highly, and write how you can leverage it to strengthen your management.

2) Consider how you need to grow in the four management skills to enhance your current and future leadership. From the previous tool, pick a self-assessment statement from each area in which you scored yourself the lowest, and briefly describe how you could improve and grow in that area to strengthen your management.

	Planning	Organizing	Guiding	Assessing
Strength to leverage				
Growth needed				

ACTION POINT: Write one step you are determined to accomplish after doing this exercise.

Development Matrix Tool

(Blends the Discover, Teach, Model, and Coach Operational Aspects)

You should develop those you lead on the basis of three things: (1) what is required of them—according to what they have been asked to do; (2) what you observe in them—according to their thinking, behavior, and skills; and (3) what they observe in themselves—according to their goals, aspirations and experiences.

1) Consider those you lead. Pick one person and brainstorm about the question, "How does that person need to develop to succeed?" Then write your ideas in the Discover row under the appropriate column.
2) Pick one idea from each of the three boxes you just filled in, and decide how you will teach, model, and coach that person in that idea.
3) Once that idea is developed in him or her, choose another idea from the top box and repeat step two. Do this for several or all people you lead.

Name:	Situation:		Time frame:
	Thinking	Behavior	Skills
Discover			
How I can help			
Teach			
Model			
Coach			

ACTION POINT: When will you review your plans with each individual?

Coach Tool #1

(Developmental Dialogue Using DRESSCODES)[33]

Use this acrostic as a guide for intentionally coaching and developing those you lead.

AREAS	POSSIBLE QUESTIONS TO ASK
Describe	Begin with an event, conversation, effort, or situation. Tell me about the _____ you had last week. How did it go? Describe it.
Role	What was your part or role in that? What were you responsible for? Describe it.
Expectation	What was your desired outcome as you began this experience? What were you hoping would happen?
Success	What went well? Why? Identify and discuss each part. What factors and people influenced that? What did you do to influence the good result?
Surprise	What surprised you? Why?
Change	What would you do differently if you could go back and start again? Why?
Observation	What did you observe about yourself as you went through this experience? How did you respond? What did you see in your leadership? ... in your emotions? ... in how you relate to others?
Development	In what areas do you sense the need to grow or develop in your leadership? ... in your skills? ... in your relationships?
Execution	How do you plan to do that? What are the next steps?
Share	Can I share a thought? (This is where you give input. Be selective and keep your remarks to just one or two things that you think will make the most difference.)

---

33 For a further development of this tool and helpful examples, see Henry Clay's book, *DRESSCODES: Developing Others through Evaluated Experience.* Used by permission. Available on Amazon.com in print and Kindle ebook.

Primary Responsibility: DEVELOP

Coach Tool #2

(Developmental Dialogue Using COACH)

Another tool for establishing a Developmental Dialogue uses the acrostic COACH (explained in the chart on the following page). Use the chart as a guide for ongoing coaching and development of those you lead. (Note: I recommend this tool for going more in-depth after initially using DRESSCODES—Coach Tool #1.)

CONCERN	OBSERVATION	ACTION	CAPACITATE	HANDSHAKE
Establish Goals	*Promote Discovery*	*Plan the Action*	*Authorize & Empower*	*Recap*
Establish Goals for the Conversation • How would you like to use our time together today? • How will you know we've accomplished that? • What is our starting point? • Where do you want to end up? • What outcome would you like from our time together? • From your point of view, what is the present situation? • Where do you want to go? To narrow the focus: • What is most urgent or important right now? • What would you like to see change? • Of the issues you raised, which is your top priority? **Establish Goals for the Long Term** • What are your long-term career aspirations? • What are some of your long-term personal aspirations? • How do these aspirations fit into your stage of life? • What legacy do you want to leave in your current role?	• What advantage is there to taking a look at this? • What have you tried and how did it make you feel? • How has this worked for you in the past? • What piece have you experimented with? • How have others responded? • When has it felt right? • What have you seen work for others? • What has challenged you the most about this? • Tell me more … • What groundwork have you done? • How is that important to you? **Types of Questions** • Observation: Who, What, When, Where? • Interpretation: What does it mean? • Correlation: Where else have we seen this? What else relates to this? • Application: What does this mean to you?	• What needs to happen? • What do you need to do to achieve your goal? • What might you try? • How else might you get to the same place? • What might happen if you explore this possibility? • What are the pluses and minuses of this approach? • How would this action contribute to achieving your goal? • What will it cost if you don't do this? • Who do you need to talk to? • Who can help you? • What is the most important thing for you to do this week? • What is the most pivotal action you could take? **Defining Limits of Authority** • Who is accountable for the successful completion of the project? • What is the scope of the project? **Establishing Checkpoints** • How often will you meet? • What type of progress report is needed? • Is this a realistic deadline? • What are you committing to do this week? **Clarifying Expectations** • What are the desired outcomes? • What level of accuracy or completeness is expected? • What requirements need to be met?	• What will be the most difficult part? • Who do you have to be for this to happen? • How will you take care of yourself? • How will others respond? • How could you sabotage yourself? • Do you need to revise any of this? • Is this a realistic deadline? • Who do you need to include or tell about this? • Who would you like me to talk to? • Who else do you need for this to happen? • What resources will you need? • What support do you need from me? • What else do you need to be successful? • What are the roadblocks you expect or need to plan for? • Are there other things that would have to change for this to happen? • What if you run into trouble?	**Looking Back** • What did you get out of our conversation today that you needed? • What are you going away with today? • What was valuable today? • Did we accomplish what you wanted to today? • What commitments were made? • What did you learn today? • What was decided? **Looking Forward** • What are you committing to do this week? • Can you check in by email and tell how it went? • What support do you need from me? • Is there anything that came up today that you want to be sure we give time to next week? • For our next meeting, what date and time will work for you? • Has anything else come to mind?

Top 12 Discovery Questions
• What do you want to have happen?
• Say more about …
• What have you already tried?
• What are the reasons this didn't work as well as you had hoped?
• How did you feel about this?
• What is your point of view?
• What are some other choices or options?
• What has worked for you in the past?
• What do you think is the most important thing to do here?
• What needs to happen in order for you to … ?
• How do you want to handle this?
• What is stopping you from moving ahead now?

Questions When You're Stuck
• What are some things you have wanted to try but haven't?
• What would you do if you had no limitations?
• If you could wave a magic wand, what would you make happen?
• What have I forgotten to ask you?
• If you were the coach, what would you ask yourself?
• If you don't know, who would know?
• In the next two years, what is the most pressing challenge or opportunity you face?
• What is the one change you can make that would have the most impact on your effectiveness as a leader?
• What's the most difficult problem you are confronting now?
• Is your current strategy/behavior working?

LEAD DEVELOP CARE

Primary Responsibility: CARE

Know Tool #1

1) Use this tool to determine how you can better know those you lead, in order to lead them better. We suggest you use one form for each person you supervise.
2) Fill in the table to the best of your knowledge. Leave blank any boxes that don't apply or that aren't appropriate based on your leadership situation.

Information you can and should know:	
Given name	
Preferred name	
Professional aspiration	
Desired area of development	
Personality type	
Strengths	
Weakness	
Motivators	
Information that may or may not be appropriate for you to know depending on the situation and relationship:	
Birthday	
Hometown	
Hobbies	

Alma mater(s)	
Issues of interest or activism	
Life story	
Skills	
Recreational activities	

Significant other	Name:	Birthday:	Anniversary:

Children	Name(s) and birthdays:
Other Information	

ACTION POINT: Determine the following two things.

1) How can you better know this person in ways that are comfortable, effective, and appropriate so that you can lead them better?

2) How and where will you confidentially store this information?

LEAD DEVELOP CARE

Know Tool #2

(Life Stages Chart)[34]

1) Using the tool on the following page, identify which column best fits your life stage as a leader.
2) Write out your initial reaction and one further question to the "Critical Question" of your stage's column.
3) Circle all the "Characteristics" from your stage's column with which you identify.
4) Circle one "Danger" that you have noticed in your life from your stage's column.
5) Looking at what you have circled, identify two "Keys" (or create your own) that could help leverage your years in this stage.

---

34 © Paul Stanley and Dave Jewitt. Used (and adapted in appearance) by permission.

LIFE STAGES

Name of Stage	LEARNING	BUILDING	FOCUSING	INVESTING
Critical Question	*Who am I?*	*Where is my place?*	*Why am I here?*	*How do I finish well and leave a legacy?*
CHARACTERISTICS	High activity Broad learning Hopeful/anxious Searching/ verifying Accomplishing Gathering Self-oriented Survival	Intense schedule Narrow leading Tyranny of the urgent Driven by expectations Improving Work-oriented Success	Changing schedule Targeted learning Uncertain/weary Second thoughts Contributing > influencing Purpose-oriented Significance	Focused/looser schedule Selected learning Anxious Accepting my role Influence > contributing Converging Others-oriented Security
DANGERS	Bad life decisions Not knowing self Pressure to "figure it out" Inadequate ambitions	No life structures Doing overrides Being Incongruency of stress Neglect of relationships	Dabbling Plateauing Change for the sake of change Prioritizing comfort and security	Stop learning and growing Lack of purpose (*rolelessness*)
KEYS TO SUCCEEDING	Exposure/ experience Understanding self Faithfulness Mentors Feedback/ adjustment Respond– learn/grow	Developing life structures Applying self Stewardship Mentors/peers Feedback/ adjustment Respond– learn/grow	Clarifying purpose Focusing self Stewardship Mentors/peers Feedback/ adjustment Respond– learn/grow	Making final years count Investing self– legacy Generosity Peers/ mentorees Feedback/ adjustment Respond– learn/grow

ACTION POINT: Adjust your monthly work flow to incorporate your keys to succeeding, and consider using a coach who can help you rethink your thinking and development.

Primary Responsibility: CARE

Connect Tool

1) Choose someone with whom you wish to connect better.
2) Answer the following questions regarding that person.

Person's name:	
What do you know about the person that will help you initiate a conversation with him or her?	
What are some things that you think you have in common with this person?	
What has this person expressed in the past (thoughts, feelings) on which you could follow up in a conversation?	
What are you willing to reveal about yourself that might further your connection with him/her?	
Based on what you know about this person, what day of the week or time of day would be best for conversing together?	

ACTION POINT: Answer the following three questions.

1) Where and when will you have the conversation?

2) What preparation do you need to do before the conversation?

3) Who will you ask, and how will you instruct him or her, to help you evaluate how well you engage and limit distractions during conversations?

Provide Tool

1) Think of a team or individual you want to evaluate regarding Provide. Fill in the top row with the applicable information.
2) In the "Current actions" column, write down the way you currently provide the things mentioned in each row.
3) Determine if your provision is sufficient in each area and indicate this (yes/no) in the next column.
4) If what you are providing is *not* sufficient, use the "Changes needed" column to plan changes that will provide the item in sufficient quantity and quality.
5) If you can, discuss this chart with someone else, and if your thoughts grow, write any further thoughts in the last column on the right.

Name:		Project/scope:		
How do you provide...	Current actions	Sufficient?	Changes needed	Further thoughts
... time?				
... attention?				
... feedback?				
... affirmation?				
... clarity?				

... physical resources?				
... immaterial resources?				
... support?				
... opportunity?				

ACTION POINT: Answer the following five questions.

1) How can you determine what the appropriate level of provision is for this person or team?

2) Are you able to provide appropriately for their success? If not, where can you find assistance?

3) Is there something you are providing that is not helpful or resulting in an over-dependence on you?

4) How will you know when you are limiting their development by providing more than you should?

5) When and where will you have a conversation with this person or team to become aligned on the appropriate levels of your provision for them? Note that when you do have this conversation, you may wish to use the items listed in the chart above as bullet points.

Protect Tool

1) Think of a team or individual that you want to evaluate regarding Protect. Fill in the information in the first row in the chart accordingly.
2) In the first open column, write down the current ways you leverage your role to protect them in a safe context regarding the things mentioned in each row.
3) In the next column state if your protection is sufficient.
4) If your protection is not sufficient, use the fourth column to plan changes that will protect them sufficiently.
5) If you can discuss this with someone else or your thoughts grow, write any further thoughts in the far-right column.

Name:			Project/scope:	
Area in which I leverage my role to provide safety	**Means by which I provide this protection**	**Sufficient?**	**Changes needed**	**Further thoughts**
A predictable work routine and environment				
A physically healthy work environment				
An emotionally healthy work environment				
Their peers (coworkers)				

My peers and supervisors				
Themselves— their view of themselves				
Themselves— personal well-being (health, family, physical activity, etc.)				
Overall context and organizational dynamics				

ACTION POINT: Answer the following three questions.

1) How can you determine what the appropriate and needed level of protection is for this person or team?

2) Are you able to sufficiently protect them so that they can succeed? If not, where can you find assistance?

3) When and where will you have a conversation with this person or team to become aligned on the appropriate level of your protection of them? You may wish to use the topics listed in the chart as bullet points in your conversation.

Intentionality and the Primary Responsibilities

1) Take a moment each month to think at a high level how you are doing in LDC with all of your direct reports. See what you notice in each of the Operational Aspects that might need attention.
2) Follow up as needed.

DATE _____

Direct Report	LEAD	DEVELOP	CARE

LDC Planning Form

Take a moment every week (even if it's just 10–12 minutes) to think about each of your direct reports in light of the Operational Aspects. This reconnects you with your intentionality toward each person. You may use this form to collect your thoughts. You don't need to fill in every box.

Name of direct report: _____ Date: _____

	Operational Aspects	Observations/ Current Activities	Next Steps
LEAD	**Set Direction**		
	Align		
	Motivate		
	Manage		
DEVELOP	**Current Developmental Focus:**		
	Discover		
	Teach		
	Model		
	Coach		
CARE	**Know**		
	Connect		
	Provide		
	Protect		

FACE Tool[35]

Use the LDC algorithm to help you process how to address a people leadership issue. Don't rush to problem solving. Seek to get a clear picture first of the main issue(s) and what part of Lead, Develop and Care will most help.

Focus: Briefly describe the situation in a couple of sentences. What do you think **the real issue** is?	
Ask: Which **Primary Responsibility** is most needed? Is it more of a Lead issue? Or Develop? Or Care? (Or a combination?) Why do you think that?	**LEAD** **DEVELOP** **CARE**
Clarify: Of that Primary Responsibility (Lead, Develop, or Care), which **Operational Aspect** is most needed (Or some combination)? Why do you think that?	**LEAD** / **DEVELOP** / **CARE** Set Direction / Discover / Know Align / Teach / Connect Motivate / Model / Provide Manage / Coach / Protect
Engage: What are some **next steps**? What is your plan? When? Who? How?	

---

35 I want to thank Chris McComb for developing this resource. Used by permission.

Using the Model: PROCESSING AS A TEAM

Think Tank

This exercise is similar to the FACE Tool, except you complete it with your team. Think Tank helps you deal with a current leadership opportunity or challenge by soliciting and incorporating team members' perspectives and ideas into your thinking. With the aid of a Moderator to guide you, you will walk through the LDC algorithm in a dynamic back-and-forth exchange to gain a clearer understanding of the leadership issue before you and to know how best to move forward.

Think Tank is designed to expand a leader's understanding and draw out ideas in a reasoned, guided, and orderly manner. Think Tank is NOT:

- Brainstorming, which involves everyone reaching into their own grab bag of tips, tricks, and previous experiences in a random scramble for possible solutions.
- Groupthink, where the most popular idea tends to become the majority view while minority views are squashed/marginalized.
- The opportunity to create a bully pulpit or a forum for humiliating individuals for their shortcomings or "development needs." (The Moderator's review of the situation in advance—including a preliminary conversation with the Chair—can help head this off from happening.)

The Roles

There are three roles in this exercise: the Chair (the person presenting the leadership opportunity or challenge—usually the "boss," the Team leader), the Team (everyone except the Chair), and the Moderator (who guides the Chair and Team through the tool; preferably someone outside the Team with as much neutrality as possible). A Moderator is needed because the tendency is to jump from a cursory understanding of a situation to "solve" the problem as quickly as possible. The Moderator prevents this truncated approach by encouraging the team to think toward the model to get at the root issues.

Additional Tips

- During the Align, Interact, and Conclude stages, the Moderator should ask questions designed to help people feel comfortable sharing a different/ dissenting view (e.g., "Several of you have said you see the main issue as a Lead issue; does anyone think it could be seen as a Develop issue? If so, why?").

- After conducting the Think Tank exercise, the Chair may or may not change how he or she sees the LDC model applied to the situation, but understanding of how everyone on the team perceives and is affected by the situation should be greater. (This helps boost a sense of Care among your team members.)

Steps to Conducting a Think Tank

Present	**Chair** briefly (1–2 minutes) describes the leadership opportunity or challenge (the issue).
Align	**Moderator** asks 2–3 other **Team** members how they heard the issue. Do they see it the same way? Why or why not? Clarify as needed between **Chair and Team.**
Interact	**Chair** explains if he/she thinks the issue is a Lead, Develop, or Care issue and why.
	Moderator asks **Team** if they agree or have a different view and why.
	Moderator asks **Chair** how his/her thoughts have been affected; **Chair** settles on the core Primary Responsibility.
	Chair explains which Operational Aspect(s) within that Primary Responsibility is (are) the focus and why.
	Moderator asks **Team** if they agree or have a different view and why.
	Moderator asks **Chair** how his/her thoughts have been affected; **Chair** settles on the core Operational Aspect(s) in play.
Conclude	**Chair** shares what he/she sees as the next steps and why.
	Moderator asks **Team** how they see the next steps and why.
	Moderator asks **Chair** how his/her thinking/ plans have been affected by the group's ideas. **Chair** settles on next steps.

**For materials and other resources,
such as online courses on the LDC framework,
please visit leaddevelopcare.com**

Acknowledgements

A heartfelt thanks to my friend and colleague Henry Clay. This has been quite a journey together. And what a special magic as we collaborated on writing the materials for the seminars over the years and around the world. I want to thank him also for his significant help with several chapters of this book. It could not have been completed without his writing abilities.

A very special thanks to Patrick Donley, Bryan Brown, and Todd Pevey. Their vision, energy, and leadership for developing and expanding our work among leaders around the world is the future.

A special thanks to Greg Nichols, who provided just what we needed with his gifts and his ability to bring added structure and organization to us.

A special thanks to Cathy Roberts, whose leadership experiences, insights, and communication skills have added so much.

A dear thanks to my friend of so many years, Jess MacCallum. His skill and talent as a graphic artist, writer, and business owner have been exceedingly helpful to us. We wouldn't be where we are today without him.

Thanks to Brian Fila—what a special friend as we walk together in shaping a different kind of leader.

Thanks to Todd Cothran—a steady friend and constant source of encouragement and much-needed nudging on writing this book!

And a very special thanks to Jenny Abel, my editor. Her ability to reshape thoughts and phrases has been amazing. What a gift to us.

Many thanks as well to Luke Forister for his great work on the graphics for this third edition.

Thanks also to Jack McQueeney, John Owen, Walt and Haley Clay, Thad McAuley, Tabita Hulaban, Wendy Clay, Abby Cook, Mike Clarke, Leanne Carter, Stan and Cheryl Burlingame, Chris Tweedy, Adam Gascho, Dwight Poggemiller, Suzy Penner, Lisa Meyers, Mike Richards,

Des Figueiredo, Alvin Edwards, Rich Bonham, Jim Hatcher, Doug Mitts, Jesse Northcutt, Jim and Sarah Meyer, John Gilberts, Howard Moore, Jerry Forte, Kelly Smith, Chris McComb, and Mark Doebler. It's been an amazing journey!

About the Author

Terry Cook is a leader, teacher, coach, and change agent. Through his passionate and skilled leadership and coaching, he has helped a wide range of individuals and organizations around the globe, from university students to leaders on Capitol Hill to agencies and leaders in the nonprofit and for-profit sectors. He regularly leads symposia that teach the LDC Leadership Model in addition to helping leaders worldwide move from cognitive knowledge to experiential understanding of the model through both onsite and virtual coaching.

Terry holds a Bachelor of Science from the University of North Texas and lives in Charlottesville, Virginia. He and his wife, Sherry, are the proud parents of four daughters and ten grandchildren. When he's not busy developing leaders, he enjoys reading, hiking, and showing family and friends the beauty of the Blue Ridge mountains.

Made in the USA
Columbia, SC
23 December 2024

50565959R00130